The Open Court
Library of Philosophy

EUGENE FREEMAN, Editor
San Jose State College

A
NATURAL THEOLOGY
FOR OUR TIME

A
NATURAL THEOLOGY
FOR OUR TIME

BY CHARLES HARTSHORNE

OPEN COURT · LA SALLE, ILLINOIS

Library of Congress Catalog Card Number: 66-14722

A NATURAL THEOLOGY FOR OUR TIME

© 1967 by The Open Court Publishing Company

Printed in the United States of America

Dedication

To the memory of Fausto Sozzini (Socinus), Italian theologian, and his brave Protestant followers in Poland and elsewhere, who in the sixteenth and seventeenth centuries were able to see and—in spite of persecution, scorn, and ridicule—to say, that the eternity or worshipful perfection of God does not imply his changelessness (or self-sufficiency) in all respects.

Also to Gustav Theodor Fechner, German physicist, psychologist, and natural theologian, and Jules Lequier, French philosopher—who, in the nineteenth century, to nearly as heedless a world, gave lucid expression to the same or related ideas.

Finally, to some philosophers writing early in the twentieth century of whom similar things could be said—for instance, Iqbal in what is now Pakistan and R. K. Mukerji in India, Varisco in Italy, Berdyaev in Russia (and

Paris), James Ward in England, and W. E.
Hocking, E. S. Brightman, W. P. Montague,
and A. N. Whitehead in the United States.

These men broke with a tradition of more
than a thousand years. Yet they were not mere
iconoclasts; they did not fall by reaction into
an opposite extreme. Seeing beyond the sterile
alternative inherited from the Greeks, "finite
God or infinite God," they envisaged the God
finite and infinite, each in suitable and clearly
distinguishable respects.

Their reward for this achievement? The
nearly complete silence or noncomprehension
of historians, encyclopedists, and textbook
writers. Nevertheless their example may give
comfort to those who would rather come as
close as possible to difficult truths than enjoy
facile half-truths in the best of company. But—
are not such men, scattered through history,
for one another the best of company?

"He will endow our fleeting days with abid-
ing worth." Jewish ritual.

Preface

The following chapters are somewhat extended and revised versions of four Morse Lectures given at Union Theological Seminary in New York, 1964. The discussions which took place after the first two lectures and a brief version of the third were very stimulating and encouraging. A new day seems to be dawning in religious thought, which for several centuries has been struggling to free itself from the intellectual chains in which Aristotelian and so-called Platonic or neo-Platonic influences have long held it confined. Some bad guesses of early secular reason, often accepted by theology as part of its own message, have been increasingly subject to criticism, both theological and philosophical. From now on, the religious idea may at last have a good chance to be judged on its merits, not on those of a spurious substitute. The philosophical 'absolute'—which Barth correctly terms a 'pagan' idea—can no longer pose unchallenged as the Worshipful One of religion.

At the same time, it begins to appear that the God of religion is in a sense more absolute than most philosophers have been prepared to admit, or most theologians to claim. For, as Anselm tried, but in part failed, to convey to scholars, the mere eternal existence of God (though not his full actuality) is, as Plato said of his Good, 'above being'—in the usual form of contingent existence. From this it follows that 'empirical' arguments for or against the divine existence are logical monstrosities. Perhaps logic is not yet ready to formulate 'exists necessarily'; but if this is the case, so much the worse for that logic's claim to completeness —should it make such a claim. A technique of reasoning which will not allow the religious idea even to be expressed is also one which cannot adjudicate the validity of that idea, except on the assumption that the adequacy of the technique for all rational purposes is to be assumed, rather than the significance and coherence of the essential idea of religion. To take *that* position is at best a personal hunch, not a rational result.

The possibility of natural theology, or a theory of divinity appealing to 'natural reason' —that is, critical consideration of the most general ideas and ideals necessary to interpret life and reality—is often said to have been thoroughly discredited by Hume and Kant. I do not share this trust in the ability of these men—whose climate of opinion was not ours—to settle for us, or for all time, the relations of theoretical reason to religion. Not details only but first principles are being reconsidered to-day, in natural science, logic, mathematics—and theology. Had they not better be reconsidered in philosophy of religion also? How 'cause', 'substance', any universal or a priori conception you please, including that of deity (which in final analysis is *the* a priori conception, summing up all the rest), should be viewed today seems to me to be our problem, not that of the giants of the 18th century.

The question of rational or natural theology, I hold, is open, not closed. Once this is granted, I am not much worried about the eventual outcome. For at least the "path of inquiry" will no longer be "barred."

Charles Hartshorne

March 5, 1965
The University of Texas

Contents

CHAPTER ONE: PHILOSOPHICAL AND RELIGIOUS
USES OF 'GOD' 1

CHAPTER TWO: THE THEISTIC PROOFS 29

CHAPTER THREE: WHY THERE CANNOT BE
EMPIRICAL PROOFS 66

CHAPTER FOUR: THEISM, SCIENCE, AND
RELIGION 90

CHAPTER FIVE: EPILOGUE: ABSTRACT AND CONCRETE
APPROACHES TO DEITY AND THE DIVINE
HISTORICITY 126

INDEX 138

Philosophical and Religious Uses of 'God'

What is a philosopher to mean by 'God'—assuming he uses the word? There are three ways of reaching an answer to this question. One is to ask theologians. But there are important disagreements among theologians as to the connotations of the central religious term, and these disagreements have if anything increased during the past century or two. Thus we cannot find an answer to the terminological question in this way. A second approach is the following. If the philosopher's system or method leads him to formulate a conception having at least some analogy with the central operative idea in the practices, not simply in the theological theories, of one or more of the high religions, he may call his conception by the religious name. If the analogy is weak he may with some justice be accused of misusing the word. Spinoza has been called "God-intoxicated" and also "atheist." There is a fairly strong case for both descriptions. But this, in my view, constitutes an objection of some force to Spinoza's system. It seems odd to think that an idea so essentially religious should be so mistakenly conceived by all the great religions concerned with it as the religious idea must be if Spinoza is correct. Contrariwise, it is an argument in favor of a philosophy if it can make more religious sense out of the theistic view than other philosophies have been able to do.

A further consideration is the following. Basic ideas derive somehow from direct experience or intuition, life as concretely lived. Moreover, it is demonstrable from almost any classical conception of God that he cannot be known in any merely indirect way, by inference only, but must somehow be present in all experience. No theist can without qualification deny the universal 'immanence' of God. Even Aquinas did not do this. And if God is in *all* things, he is in our experiences and also in what we experience, and thus is in some fashion a universal datum of experience. But then it seems reasonable to suppose that religion, whatever else it may be, is the cultivation of this aspect of experience. Hence what it says about 'God' deserves to be taken seriously, at least so far as the meaning of the term is concerned. The burden of justification is upon those who would use the word in a drastically nonreligious sense. So our first question is, what is the religious sense?

In theistic religions God is the One Who is Worshipped. This is in some sort a definition. We have, therefore, only to find out what worship is to know the proper use of the name 'God'. This is the third approach to the definitional problem. But here, too, a difficulty arises. Are there not many sorts of worship— noble, ignoble, primitive, sophisticated, superstitious, relatively enlightened, idolatrous . . . what you will? And does not divinity take on a different apparent character with each form of worship? Spinoza claimed to have the noblest and most enlightened form of worship, the "intellectual love of God"; hence to require him to refrain from using the word because other, perhaps less enlightened, people worship differently may be to rule against enlightenment and in favor of vulgar superstition. Moreover, the mere fact that many, or even most, people (at least in certain cultures) have worshipped God in a certain way is nothing but a contingent empirical fact. Should we allow our view concerning the essential nature of the eternal deity to depend upon any such facts? All classical meanings treat God as in some sense eternal. How can there be valid inference from a mere temporal fact to truth about eternal things? Much less could counting noses determine such truth.

If worship is to be definitive of deity, it must be worship as more than a mere fact of terrestrial human culture. The definitional problem has a clear solution only if there is a rationale, an inner logic, to the *idea* of worship such that inferior forms violate or fail adequately to express this logic. And it cannot be a rationale of worship as a mere terrestrial phenomenon, but must concern an a priori possibility for rational animals generally, on no matter what planet, and even in no matter what possible world. Indeed, we do not have to say 'animal', for there is a sense in which God can worship, that is, worship himself. But only God can in the full sense *be* worshipped.

To obtain a broad perspective we may remind ourselves that subrational animals, below the level of language, can scarcely be thought to worship, unless in some radically deficient sense. Only man, among this earth's inhabitants, is a 'religious animal'. This suggests that consciousness, in the sense requiring language (or else, if God is conscious, something superior to language), is part of the definition of worship. To worship is to do something consciously. To do what? That which all sentient individuals must do, at least unconsciously, so far as they are sane and not in at least a mild neurosis or psychosis. Worship is the *integrating* of all one's thoughts and purposes, all valuations and meanings, all perceptions and conceptions. A sentient creature feels and acts as one, its sensations and strivings are all *its* sensations and strivings. So are its thoughts, if it has them. Thus one element of worship is present without worship, unity of response. The added element is consciousness: worship is a consciously unitary response to life. It lifts to the level of explicit awareness the integrity of an individual responding to reality. Or, worship is individual wholeness flooded with consciousness. This is the ideal toward which actual worship may tend.

If this account is correct, worship is in principle the opposite of a primitive phenomenon. The more consciousness, the more completely the ideal of worship can be realized. Those who pride themselves on transcending worship may only be falling back to a more primitive level. Of course, as many are fond of reminding us, one can live without worship. Why not, since the lower animals do so? And we are all animals; the animal way is partly open to us still.

However, there are two possible theories of worship, the theistic and the nontheistic. According to the former, the conscious wholeness of the individual is correlative to an inclusive wholeness in the world of which the individual is aware, and this wholeness is deity. According to the nontheistic view, either there is no inclusive wholeness, or if there is one, it is not what religions have meant by deity. Perhaps it is just The Unknown, or Nature as a Great Mystery, not to be thought of as conscious, or as an individual in principle superior to all others. Perhaps it is even Humanity. Or (more reasonably) it is all sentient creatures.

My view I shall put bluntly. It is the lower animals for whom the Whole must be simply Unknown, sheer Mystery, and their own species practically all that has value. The difference between agnostics (or 'humanists') and the nonspeaking creatures is that, whereas the mere animal simply *has* integrity, the agnostic feels the need and possibility of raising integrity to the conscious level, but does not quite know how to do so. Thus he is in some degree in conflict with himself. However, animal innocence is there to fall back upon.

God is the wholeness of the world, correlative to the wholeness of every sound individual dealing with the world. Note that this has no peculiar connection with the human race, 'father-images', the parental function, or anything of the sort. Any sentient individual in any world experiences and acts as one: the question is if its total environment is not therewith experienced as, in some profoundly analogous sense, one. An individual (other than God) is only a fragment of reality, not the whole; but is *all* individuality (in other than the trivial sense in which a junk pile, say, is an 'individual' junk pile) similarly fragmentary? Or is the cosmic or all-inclusive whole also an integrated individual, the sole non-fragmentary individual?

Note, too, that our question is definitely not the question, 'Are all wholes or individuals "finite", "limited"?' For it is at best a leap in the dark to assert the nonfinitude of our *total* environment (or "all with which we have to do"—as W. E. Hocking puts it). This totality is vastly more than, and includes, ourselves; but it may for all that be finite in certain respects. Indeed, it must be so! Fragmentariness, not finitude, sets the problem of worship. Here countless theologians long ago made an initial mistake for which the full price has yet to be paid: they began the idolatrous worship of 'the infinite'. Cosmic wholeness, not infinity, is the essential concept. Infinity comes in if and only if—or in whatever sense and only that sense—we should view the whole as infinite. And this is to be determined by inquiry, not taken for granted.

The reader may feel that we have not followed our own injunction to look to the religions for the meaning of 'God'. Is 'cosmic wholeness' a religious conception? My reply is, by fairly clear and direct implication, yes, it is such a conception. I shall now try to show this. Three religions, if no more, Judaism, Christianity, and Islam would, I think, agree with the conception of worship embodied in: "Thou shalt love the Lord thy God with all

thy heart and with all thy mind and with all
thy soul and with all thy strength." I ask, how
more plainly could the idea of wholeness of
individual response be stated in simple, generally intelligible language? The word 'all' reit-
erated four times in one sentence means, I take
it, what it says. It does not mean, *nearly* all—
or, all *important*—responses, or aspects of personality. Simply every response, every aspect,
must be a way of loving God. That the God
correlative to this integrity of response is Himself 'One' or individual is also a Jewish-
Christian-Islamic tenet, at least apart from the
subtleties of the Trinity, which are surely not
intended to contradict the divine wholeness or
integrity.

But, perhaps you say, the God of the religions mentioned is not the cosmic *whole:* he
is only the cosmic creator. This 'only' suggests
that there could be more than God! Or is God
more than the all-inclusive reality? Yet this
is nonsense. Thus we seem to have a severe
paradox or dilemma. Are the basic religious
writings responsible for this paradox? True,
the Bible, for instance, nowhere says in so
many words that God is the whole of things,
but no more does it say that he is not the
whole. The 'pantheistic' issue had not arisen,
and so the wrong solution could not yet be
given. (We so easily forget that our sophisti-
cation is a danger as well as an opportunity.)
Of course "no graven image" of God was per-

mitted, but what sculptor knows how to image
the whole of things? What is there in the Bible
to show that the word 'God' refers to less than,
or even other than, the all-inclusive reality—
except a few passages which would discom-
fort traditional theists as much as they would
any pantheist, e.g., "God walked in the gar-
den." And Paul says that we live, move, and
have our being "in" God. Precisely.

Ah, you say, but the religious God is creator,
and 'X creates Y' contradicts 'Y is in X'. Does
it indeed? In that case no man can create his
own thoughts, and a poet does not create the
verbal images which constitute lines of his
poem before he writes them down. And if you
say, but of course divine creating has nothing
in common with human creating, then I ask
how the word 'create' can be a human word?
Or, if you say, but God creates free, self-active
individuals other than himself, and this the
human thinker or poet does not do, I am still
not greatly impressed. For one thing, a human
child grows new nerve or brain cells for a time
after birth, and even an adult perpetually
grows new cells of many kinds; and these cells
are living individuals which remain in the
child or adult. (That they have some slight
freedom of action I cannot empirically prove
and the reader cannot disprove.) For another
thing, either a poet does ultimately create something in other individuals, or he writes in vain.

Still more obviously, a teacher, parent, or friend creates important elements in the personalities of pupils, children, or friends. Is there an absolute difference between this and divine creating? If you say that God—and he alone—creates the entire personality of a man, you seem to leave nothing for the man to create in himself, and then when we say, as it is good idiom to say, that a man 'makes' a decision or an effort, we do not know what we are talking about. Not much is left of personality if we abstract from all the past decisions and efforts which the individual has himself made. Sartre's phrase for man, *causa sui,* needs qualification, but is not wholly wrong. And, once more, if no human making has relevance to God's making of the world, the latter phrase is mere equivocation, indeed gibberish.

But now probably you are about to overwhelm me with an inconsistency. For what the poet, teacher, parent, or friend makes in another human being does not become a constitutive element within the first human being, the maker. And I have been saying that what God makes in us does become a constitutive element in him. My defense, however, is not so difficult. For is it absolutely, or only relatively, true that what we make in others fails to become part of our own reality? If only relatively true, then it is not absolutely false to say that it becomes such a part. And then the corresponding affirmation need not be false at all of God.

Let us consider this further. If a pupil listens in silence to a teacher, absorbing valuable ideas but never communicating the changes in himself to the teacher, who never learns the results of his teaching, then indeed it seems that what is created in the pupil remains outside the teacher. But suppose the latter intimately follows the pupil's mental growth and personality changes. Can we then say that these, his own creations in the pupil's mind, in no degree become constitutive of the teacher's mind? For instance, the teacher shares sympathetically in the pupil's excitement over ideas new to him, enjoys the nuances of his emotional and intellectual responses to the ideas. Is not his own life thereby enriched? Consider also that when we speak of the teacher's "following with sympathetic understanding" the pupil's responses we are talking about fallible human operations. The teacher does not entirely understand or altogether sympathetically follow. By contrast, if God knows the results in us of his creative actions upon us, he knows and shares them with a completeness, an intimacy, compared to which our knowledge is always partial and external. The pupil remains indeed outside the human teacher, and by the same token much in the pupil remains hidden from the teacher. It even remains more or less hidden from the pupil, much of whose reality can be said to be outside his own clearly conscious experience. Omniscience, if the term is to have human meaning, must not be absolutely different from our knowing; but still, it must somehow differ in principle from ours. The clue to this likeness and this difference is in our hands: God is the all-inclusive reality; his knowing, accordingly, must likewise be all-inclusive; ours, by contrast, is fragmentary, as our whole being is fragmentary; much remains outside us as knowers. Strange that men should think to exalt God by putting everything outside him as knower. Almost everything is outside us and our knowledge; that is why we are not God! But nothing can be outside God, in his total reality. Thus when God creates, he creates additional contents of his own awareness, enriches the panorama of existence as his to enjoy.

The idea that worship is love with the whole of one's being is correlated, in many high religions, with the idea that what we thus wholly love is itself also love, the divine love for all creatures, and for God himself as including all. And this in my opinion is not simply a pretty sentiment but is, in cold logic, the most rational way to view the matter. Two reasons among many for this belief:

(1) It seems impossible to love an unloving being with all one's own being. For instance, if we cannot entirely avoid self-love (and we cannot), then in loving the object of all our love must we not somehow be loving ourselves? The same is true of love for our friend or neighbor. But how can these loves be elements in our love for God? Only if the inclusive referent of our concern Himself cherishes all creatures, only if he loves all-inclusively, is the puzzle solved. Only supreme love can be supremely lovable.

(2) What is concrete knowledge, knowledge inclusive of the actual concrete feeling of creatures, if not some kind of sympathetic participation or love? Must not God, as the well-integrated whole of things, have such knowledge? Mere intellect cannot know concrete qualities of feeling, for they are not concepts, abstract forms or patterns, and no mere form or pattern can contain them in their fullness. If God knows but does not love, this means either that he is indifferent to, or that he hates, what he knows. But the first is an impossible psychology. One knows only that in which one takes some sort of interest; we, for instance, know the actual feelings of others because we have at least an unconscious, or even instinctive and animal, sympathy with these feelings. What reason is there to suppose that to speak of purely nonemotional knowledge of particu-

lar emotions in their concrete uniqueness is
anything but gibberish or contradiction? One
may classify emotions relatively unemotion-
ally, but classification is precisely not knowing
the concrete in its concreteness. And only
those who feel some emotions can even classify
them and know what they are doing.

If God cannot be indifferent to creaturely
feelings, he also cannot hate them. For God
is inclusive and hate is exclusive. It is saved
from complete blindness only because there
is, as subtle psychologists have long known,
an element of love in it. There is also an element of self-conflict in hate which would contradict any classical religious idea of God.

If I am right, is it not odd that the Greeks
were so nearly unable to conceive love as a
divine quality? Plato almost managed to do it,
in saying that God created because he was
not jealous or stingy, and was willing to have
others enjoy the blessings of existence. But he
put it strangely negatively. Why? Apparently
because he was partly trapped (as Aristotle
was wholly trapped) in the verbal confusion:
God is worshipped because he is complete,
perfect, free of any defect, hence he is immutable and incapable of wishing for any good
not already possessed; 'love', on the contrary,
means desire for the not yet attained. Hence,
Plato thought—and *a fortiori* Aristotle thought
—the ultimate object of love must be quite

other than love. It must be absolute beauty,
sheer excellence, stilling all longing for anything further. But neither Plato nor anyone else
has been able to show us how there can be a
beauty or excellence inclusive of all value
whatever, unless it be the beauty of a love
which cherishes all valuable, beautiful, or loving creatures. Beauty as a value is actualized
only in experience. However, the concrete
beauty of the cosmos—and a mere abstraction
cannot be the inclusive object of interest—
could not be adequately appreciated by our
fragmentary kind of perception and thought.
There can then be an all-inclusive beauty only
if there be an all-inclusive appreciation of
beauty, and what could that be if not a cosmic
sympathy? Cosmic beauty as a value must be
actualized in cosmic experience, and this, as
we have shown, can only be a cosmic love.

If such a love must in some sense be incom-
plete and mutable, so much the worse for the
identification of the One Worshipped with the
complete or immutable. Our love for God is
not immutably complete and should not be;
for it includes new responses to neighborly
needs which are changing from moment to
moment. Also our total environment, that
with which we have to deal, is mutable. It is
complete, finished once for all, only if it be
correct to view future events as no less determinate than past events—a view which is at

best paradoxical. Should religion be saddled from the outset and by definition with this paradox? I think not. The idea of worship as conscious integrity, achieved through an inclusive integral object of love, does not of itself commit us to the immutable completeness of the One Who is Inclusively Loved. If anything, it conflicts with this idea, for who knows what love could be, combined with immutability? Were the Greeks not right as to that?

Not completeness, but all-inclusiveness, is what is required. And here nontheistic theories of worship fail. 'Humanity' leaves a vast world outside. Consider for example, the quintillions of singing birds which have lived and died where no man heard them sing, or the other habitable planets, the nonexistence of which we have no right to assume. If God, or the One Worshipped, does not include these, then in being even slightly interested in them we are doing something besides loving God.

It is not enough to say, "But we thank God for creating them." God, qua creator-of-X, either does or does not include X. If he does, my point is granted. If he does not, then in thinking this very thought I have gone beyond loving God to loving (or being mildly interested in) certain individuals outside him. But then my total interest is not in God, but only a part of my interest.

I conclude that the wholeness view of worship and of the divine correlate of worship makes good religious sense and is more obviously relevant to the religious documents than the identification of deity with the infinite, absolute, unconditioned (*pace* Tillich), immutable, uncaused cause, most real being, or kindred philosophical objects. If Spinoza had asserted only that all things are in and constitutive of deity, he would not have been an 'atheist' at all. But he also asserted the absolute infinity, impassibility, and noncontingency of deity, and these ideas (not merely these terms) are not religious. He identified the all-inclusive divineness with sheer infinity, necessity, or nonreceptivity, and this, so far as religion is concerned, is at best a leap in the dark.

There is another way, besides using the ideas of all-inclusiveness and universal love, to define the One Who is Worshipped. This third way was Anselm's discovery (though Philo and others almost anticipated him)—a stroke of genius even apart from its use in the ontological argument. God is the not conceivably surpassable being. For, if God could be surpassed by a greater or better, should we not worship the one who would surpass him— even were this but a conceivable not an actual being? Also, in merely thinking about the better possible being our interest would go beyond God to something else, and we should not be able to obey the Great Commandment of total devotion to the One Being.

But Anselm spoiled his formula by his way of construing it. He supposed that it was equivalent to the standard definition in terms of immutable perfection. It is indeed so equivalent if, but only if, we take 'unsurpassable' to mean 'by any being, even the being itself'. For there are two ways of being surpassed: by another, and by self. An individual can be or become superior to itself, without—so far as anyone has shown—this necessarily entailing, even as a possibility, that another than itself should surpass it. Anselm's mind, however, was full of the Greek glorification of the immutable; he accepted the Platonic-Aristotelian argument that what is worshipful must be self-sufficient and perfect in the sense of complete, and that what is complete cannot change —obviously not for the better, and surely not for the worse. Change is a sign of weakness, it was thought, and its only value must be to remedy a prior defect. But there is nothing in the religions (unless in Hinduism or Buddhism) to indicate that change simply as such is a weakness; and the only sense in which 'perfection' is used biblically is the ethical sense. "Be ye perfect" does not mean, 'be ye immutable'! Nor is any immutability attributed to deity in the Scriptures save what the context implies is purely ethical. A fixity of ethical principles is one thing, a fixity of a being's whole perceptive-conscious reality is another, and worlds apart from the first. I hope this seems as clear to the reader as it does to me, that is to say, very clear indeed.

Perfection taken as an absolute maximum does exclude change, as well as any possibility of being surpassed by another. But the converse deduction, of the absolute maximum from unsurpassability by another, succeeds only if we assume that what is unsurpassable by another must be unsurpassable by self as well. And this assumption is not self-evident; if anything, it is clearly false, as we shall see. Granted that what can be surpassed, even if only by self, is not an absolute maximum of value or reality. Granted further that *if* such a maximum is conceivable, then any self-surpassing being must fall short of this maximum, and so it could be surpassed by a being which possessed the maximum. On that basis the self-surpassing must also be conceivably surpassable by another. But is an absolute maximum conceivable? The truth is that our ancestors had not yet learned our hard modern lessons concerning the ease with which grammatically smooth expressions—class of all classes, for example—can fall into implicit contradiction or nonsense. 'Greatest possible number' is grammatical, but it is sheer nonsense if it means 'greatest finite number'; it is also, according to some mathematicians, nonsense if it means 'greatest infinite number'; and it is at best problematic, according to any mathematician. Why then should 'greatest possible value' be regarded as safe? It is vaguer, but perhaps only because it has no definite meaning at all.

Since it is at best doubtful that 'X is in all respects maximal' expresses a coherent idea, we cannot infer 'surpassable by another' from 'surpassable by self'. Moreover, our idea of wholeness throws a clear light on how 'self-surpassing' can be combined with 'unsurpassability by another'. For, if a being is in principle, or without possible failure, all-inclusive, then any possible rival could only be one of its own possible constituents, and so not a rival after all. For this to hold, God must be viewed as *necessarily* all-inclusive, incapable of a genuinely 'external' environment. Anselm, rightly, I hold, argued that the very existence of the unsurpassable being must be necessary.

A being necessarily all-inclusive must be one whose potentiality for change is coextensive with the logically possible. I call this property 'modal coincidence'. All actual things must be actual in God, they must be constituents of his actuality, and all possible things must be potentially his constituents. He is the

Whole in every categorial sense, all actuality in one individual actuality, and all possibility in one individual potentiality. This relatively simple idea was apparently too complex for most of our ancestors to hit upon. They did not reject it, they failed so much as to formulate it. (Exceptions are relatively little-known figures in the history of philosophy and theology, and even they were not too explicit about it. Plato, with his World Soul doctrine, is the nearest to an illustrious exception.)

Modal coincidence implies that the traditional identification of deity with infinity was a half truth. All-possibility—which is indeed infinite if anything is—coincides with divine potentiality. Thus, God is infinite in what he could be, not in what he is; he is infinitely capable of actuality, rather than infinitely actual. Not that he thus lacks an infinity which some conceivable being might have, but that an 'absolutely infinite or unsurpassable maximum of actuality' makes no sense. Possibility is in principle inexhaustible; it could not be fully actualized. Actuality and finitude belong together, possibility and infinity belong together. (This may not be quite all that needs to be said about their relations, but it is a good part of what needs to be said.)

We have so far justified our explication of 'God' or 'deity' with reference to religions other than those of East Indian origin. Is not

Buddhism atheistic, and yet a way of reaching individual wholeness? And does not Hinduism admit God only as an inferior manifestation of the mysterious Ultimate? These are subtle questions. There is no doubt that Buddhism, at least in the Northern form, aims at and claims to reach an experience of oneness with all things. How close this comes to theism varies in different sects. Suzuki once said that it comes very close in Zen. My contention is simply this: Buddhism does not offer an explicit alternative to the theistic version of the all-inclusive reality; rather the Buddhist refuses to rationalize what is given in 'satori' or salvation. His doctrine is an intuitionism, not a speculative account of the Whole. (To identify this intuitionism with Western 'scientific naturalism' is, I should think, arbitrary in the extreme.) Buddhism is rather a renunciation of theorizing than a theoretical rival to theism. (And it certainly is not natural science. Supernatural overtones are pervasive in Buddhist writings, even though one cannot readily articulate them conceptually.) Metaphysics, being an attempt to theorize about first principles, does not face a choice between theism and Buddhistic nontheism. The only clear-cut metaphysical theory in Buddhism is its analysis of 'substance' into unit-events or momentary states. This analysis Western metaphysics may well take seriously and even in large part ac-

cept. But the question of deity is not thereby
answered. Whitehead, granted a rather simple
correction of his analysis, has shown how God
can be conceived in these terms.

As for Hinduism, it tends, like Buddhism,
"when the chips are down" to renounce theory
for sheer intuition. The contrast between Maya,
correlative to ignorance, and Reality, correlative to true knowledge, resists conceptual analysis. Is Maya a form of being (and what
form?), a form of nonbeing, a mixture of being and nonbeing, neither being nor nonbeing?
The question is put, but orthodox exponents are
coy with the answer. The analogies, such as
the rope seeming to be a snake, are not concepts but extremely vague suggestions. We are
told that, as a dream is cancelled by waking
and finding it was but a dream, so Maya is
cancelled by waking to True Reality. But in
sober truth dreams, like ropes, are not cancelled.
They remain just as real events as waking experiences. True, what they seemed to reveal
concerning the rest of the world may have been
largely (though never, as could be shown,
wholly) mistaken, but if so the mistakes were
really made. It will never be true that they
were not made. And the rope was also really
there. Press any statement by the followers of
Sankara and you find, I am convinced, that
the semblance of conceptual definiteness and
logical structure is itself Maya. Or, if there is

an intellectual doctrine other than the renunciation of intellect, it is the familiar Western
doctrine (as in Plotinus) of 'the absolute', the
formless 'infinite', viewed as superior to, but
manifested in, all definite, finite actuality, even
divine actuality. This doctrine I hold is an intellectual as well as religious mistake. Only
potentiality can be strictly infinite, nonrela-
tive, and immutable; actuality, which is richer
than potentiality, is finite, relative, and in process of creation. God as actual is more than
the absolute (which indeed is a mere abstraction), not less.

I am open to conviction in these matters,
but my trouble can hardly be a result of not
having read enough Hindu philosophy. For
there have been and are learned thinkers in
India who have said much the same thing as
I have just done. Eventually we may all, in
East and West, hope to reach better understanding concerning the role of logic in religious thought. Intuition is valuable, and indeed indispensable; but I have a certain faith
in the rights and duties of rational metaphysical inquiry, and I shall give up this faith only
when the inevitable failure of rational metaphysics has been shown in some more con-
clusive way than by arguing ad nauseam from
the difficulties of certain traditional forms of
metaphysics whose failure I admit from the
outset.

In what kind of philosophy is the religious idea of God most at home?

(1) It must be a philosophy in which becoming is not considered inferior to being. For the self-surpassing divinity is in process of surpassing itself, and if the supreme reality is thus a supreme process, lesser individual realities will be instances of an inferior form of process. Being can then be no more than an abstraction from becoming.

(2) It must be a philosophy which avoids declaring all individual existence to be contingent. For God, to be unsurpassable by others, must exist necessarily. Yet at the same time all actuality must indeed be contingent, even divine actuality, for the latter includes all contingent things. It follows that we need a philosophy which distinguishes between the bare or abstract truth that an individual exists and the how or actual concrete state in which it exists. Individual self-identity must be granted a certain independence from concrete actuality. Philosophies which clearly provide for this are of the Buddhist-Whiteheadian type, according to which the most concrete mode of reality is not existing substance, thing, or person, but actually occurring event, state, or experience.

(3) A theistic philosophy must be in some sense indeterministic. It must admit (as Hume and Kant would not) that process is creative

of novelty that is not definitely implicit in the
antecedent situation. For otherwise only ignorance would make self-surpassing seem real;
while for God past, present, and future would
form but a single perpetually complete reality.
And this, we have seen, is not the religious
view. Also a deterministic theory of temporal
process implies theologically either a denial of
all contingency, as in Spinoza, or an absolutely
mysterious nontemporal freedom (at least for
God), as in Kant.

(4) A theistic philosophy must take 'create'
or 'creator' as a universal category, rather
than as applicable to God alone. It must distinguish supreme creativity from lesser forms
and attribute some degree of creativity to all
actuality. It must make of creativity a 'transcendental', the very essence of reality as self-
surpassing process. This is precisely what
Whitehead does in his "category of the ultimate" (Chapter 2 of *Process and Reality*).

(5) A theistic philosophy must have a theory
of internal relations and also a theory of external relations. Of internal relations, for a
whole logically requires its constituents and
God in his concrete actuality being the inclusive whole requires all things; moreover, the
creatures require God as the correlate of their
own integrity. In some deficient sense the creatures include God, as well as God the creatures.
Finally, any creative act requires its anteced-

ent data. Of external relations, for though God in his particular or contingent actuality includes all actuality, yet in his bare individual existence as the divine being and no other he—and he alone—is necessary, and what is necessary cannot include, or be constituted by, relation to anything contingent. Only the contingent can be relative. Hence the abstract necessary aspect of God does not include the actual world, and is not relative to it. (In addition, the antecedent data of a creative synthesis are independent of the synthesis.) Both types of relations are provided for by Whitehead's theory of 'prehensions' and the two 'natures' of God.

With these requirements in mind I ask you, Was it any such doctrine as this 'neoclassical theism' (as I call it) which Hume and Kant evaluated in their alleged refutations of all natural theology? Or were they—and especially, perhaps, Kant—as unaware as any child that such a doctrine could be formulated and seriously defended? I confess I find the latter view to fit the known facts. Kant, at least, did not so much as dream of neoclassical theism, or the metaphysics which can adequately express it. If then he refuted the doctrine, this was indeed a stupendous achievement, an amazing piece of luck or feat of divination. But did he refute it? I fail altogether to see that he did.

Perhaps there is one qualification: the first

Antinomy might be thought to be such a refutation, provided one accepts the finitistic trend in mathematics as authoritative. In the present work this matter must remain unfinished business.

There seems to be no equally clear religious alternative to theistic metaphysics, defined as belief in the modally all-inclusive or nonfragmentary being, surpassable only by Himself. These characterizations spring much more directly from the ideal of worship than terms like 'absolute', 'infinite', 'immutable', 'unconditioned', and similar legacies from Aristotle, Philo, Plotinus, or Plato badly understood. How different intellectual history might have been had we not been saddled so long with these pseudo-platonic simplifications! However, as a politician once remarked, "the future is before us."

In the next chapter I shall give some indications of the manner in which the theistic proofs can be reformulated to fit the new situation in the philosophy of religion, a situation—to repeat—of which Hume and Kant were scarcely able even to dream.

CHAPTER TWO

The Theistic Proofs

That the classical proofs for the divine existence failed is one of the most widely-held philosophical convictions. I agree that the proofs failed; but I find the customary explanations of how and why they did so inadequate and, in part, quite erroneous. And I insist that it was the classical proofs which failed, not all possible theistic proofs, so that the impossibility of proof has not been established.

One trouble with the customary accounts, whether those given by natural theologians or even, to some extent, by their critics, is a naive notion of what a proof in principle ought to amount to. It was thought that a proof would be a set of undeniable or axiomatic premises from which the desired conclusion could be deduced. Today we realize that axiomatic status is a relative and more or less subjective matter. Scarcely anything of importance is axiomatic for everyone. As for deduction, what it does is to establish a price for rejecting its conclusions. Suppose P entails Q. Then those who initially accept P must either accept Q also, or reconsider their acceptance of P. The mere entailment relation is of course neutral between these two procedures. Of what use then is formal argument in natural theology? Will not all who doubt the conclusion transfer their doubt to the premises? Some will do so, but all—that may be open to question. Here, as often, there are two opposing extremes and an intermediate position. (In this I am indebted to Dr. George Mavrodes.) Human beings are unlikely (at least in anything like their present state of culture) to find premises acceptable to everyone from which theism can validly be deduced. No matter what theistic argument is offered, some will hold the premises no less doubtful than the conclusion. But though it is unrealistic to hope that all doubts concerning theism can be removed by deductive argument, it may be quite as unrealistic to suppose that no doubts can be removed. In the past many people have felt that certain premises which they thought entailed the divine existence were more convincing than the simple affirmation of that existence by itself. It is very clear to me that I should not have been a theist all these

years had I not found the *P*'s which I take to
entail this *Q* to be such that their denial is for
me much more clearly counterintuitive than
the simple rejection of *Q*.

Of course, from a lofty point of view, formal
proofs are but crutches, aids to our weak human insights. Were we less weak and confused
we should simply see the truth, and that would
be the end of the matter. But crutches for the
weak can be very useful. It may be a good
deal easier to see a truth if its logical con-
nections with various propositions, initially not
known to be connected with it, are made clear.
The glib denial of this is unreasonable. The
popularity of the denial seems to derive partly
from the wish of some that theism should not
find rational support because they prefer to go
on disbelieving it, and partly from the wish of
others that it should not find rational support
because, they think, belief should be independent of secular reason and thus remain in the
hands of preachers and theologians, or to speak
more generously, belief should be a matter of
faith. "Blessed are the pure in heart for they
shall see God." Never mind the reasoners, unless they too are pure in heart—and then their
reason is not to the point. But how many persons are so very pure that they can believe
even if they are aware that no reasoner thinks
that reasoning favors belief? And ought they
to believe, on that supposition? I incline to

think (with Freud, for example) that the impossibility of any rational argument for belief, supposing it really obtained, would be a strong and quite rational argument *against* belief. I suspect that most unbelievers agree with me here. And so, officially, does the Roman Catholic Church.

In considering proofs we must realize that if proofs have premises, so—unless they are purely and trivially formal—do criticisms of proofs. For one thing, critics have generally supposed that the theologians knew their business in defining the theism they wished to justify. Thus Kant supposes that the problem is to establish "a most real being," wholly infinite, timeless, and absolute. But if our previous chapter was soundly argued, this is a basic though theologically popular mistake. Furthermore, since divinity is not religiously conceived as a mere illustration of first principles but as somehow *the* first principle, the correlate of every interest and every meaning, it follows that any metaphysical assumption implicitly either expresses or contradicts theism. It cannot be neutral toward it if it is on the metaphysical level of generality. Only empirical issues are thus neutral. Hence no theistic view can be criticized without at least implicit metaphysical commitments.

Kant's rejection of rational theology affirms or assumes a metaphysics (or if you prefer,

an antimetaphysics) which is radically antitheistic (as I have defined theism). It is not
merely neutral or agnostic. Thus the procedure
does what the proofs are accused of doing. It
reaches a controversial conclusion by reasoning from premises equally controversial. Some
of Kant's initial assumptions—I could give
quite a list of them—are to me, as a theist, no
less counterintuitive than his conclusion that
there can be no rational argument for belief.
The invalidity of classical proofs is not all that
would follow from these assumptions; rather
they imply the absurdity of theism itself even
as affirmed by faith. What Kant cogently refuted were only propositions that rational theology has no need to affirm. And, insofar as
his argument touches the truly theistic conception, it is as question-begging as it well could
be. The same is true of Hume, though his antitheistic assumptions were only in part the same.
(See the discussions of Hume and Kant in my
book *Anselm's Discovery,* Open Court, 1965.)
Thus the whole episode is a detour. It is time
to return to the highway.

All rational argument presupposes rules,
universal principles. From the merely particular or specific nothing can be deduced. Yet
how can there be principles applicable to God?
Is he not the Great Exception? Why otherwise
should we worship him? A case under a rule
is *a* case, one among others, comparable to

others; but God must be *sui generis,* the only possible worshipful being. From this point of view, it seems not enough to say that God is the 'supreme' being; we must, it seems, go further, and with Tillich deny that God is *a* being. Rather, he is "being itself." Also God does not 'exist', for it is beings which exist. But alas, we now seem to have made deity a mere universal, wholly lacking in concrete or particular actuality. Rightly does Niebuhr fear that in this doctrine Greek abstractionism triumphs over Christian concreteness and appreciation of individual uniqueness. I hold with Niebuhr here.

Two requirements, seemingly opposed, must be met if natural theology is to be in any degree possible. God must, in spite of all difficulties, be a case under rules, he must be an individual being. However, he must not be a mere, even the greatest, individual being; rather, he must also in some fashion coincide with being or reality as such or in general. And here I accuse Tillich of a subtle form of the very error he is trying to avoid, that of putting God under an inappropriate rule. It is a rule universally valid except with reference to deity that what is individual is not, to an equal degree, universal, and what is universal is not to an equal degree individual. Individuality and universality ordinarily are opposed. They are not entirely opposed—and this is important—

in that, for example, a man's distinctive personality traits are a sort of highly specific universals of which each momentary state of the
man is a new instance or embodiment. Still,
apart from God, an individual is a far cry from
anything so general as reality itself or as such.
What Tillich overlooks, however, is that this
seemingly inevitable contrast between universality and individuality is one of the very rules
to which God as worshipful or unsurpassable
must be an exception. His uniqueness must
consist precisely in being both reality as such
and an individual reality, insofar comparable
to other individuals.

It is clearly nonsense to declare an entity
wholly incomparable and yet compare it to
all others as their superior. And if not superior,
it is not worshipful! Nor can we look up to mere
colorless 'being' or reality. God is "the most
high" or the most excellent one, and this means
that he can and must be compared to others.
Yet he is also incomparable. Tillich, in accept-
ing the incomparability and rejecting the com-
parability, is giving us a half truth, and is
missing the point no less than are those who
suppose God to be the greatest individual being
and *therefore* in no sense as universal as being
itself. The Worshipful One is not simply the
most excellent individual, but he is that. One
may even say that what is incomparable about
God is just that he is both comparable and in-

comparable, whereas other individuals are merely comparable. This is a formula translatable into many equivalents. Thus God is not simply infinite, or "wholly other" than finite things; nor is he simply one more, though the greatest, finite thing: rather he and he alone is both finite and infinite, and likewise: both relative and absolute, conditioned and unconditioned, mutable and immutable, contingent and necessary. He is individual, but *the individual with strictly universal functions,* the all-encompassing and yet not merely universal principle of existence.

This is exactly the point of theism: that the ultimate principle is individual, not a mere or universal form, pattern system, matter, or force—or that, conversely, the ultimate individual is strictly universal in its scope or relevance. A human individual is not the very principle of existence; of course not, for he is not the Unsurpassable, he is not God. But a mere universal, even 'being' or 'reality' simply as universal, also cannot be God, who must be the most individual of universals, the most universal of individuals. This may suggest Hegel's "concrete universal," but is really quite different, the point being that individuality is one thing and concreteness or 'actuality' quite another. The same thing can be both universal and individual, but that universality and concreteness should be coincident is mere contradiction. God is both universal and concrete; but the concreteness transcends the universality and is incomparably more than God merely as existing or individual. One must admit a real distinction (real for God, not just for us) between abstract individuality or existence (these are the same) and full concrete actuality (which is quite different). Neoclassical theism is not Hegelian, though it may have learned something from Hegel.

But now, if we must thus make deity an exception even to the rule that individuality and universality are opposed, what rules shall we use in reasoning about theism? This is *the* question of natural theology, and one not clearly envisaged in the classical discussions. Not having been envisaged it can hardly have been answered.

If the idea of God is to have a rational place among our ideas, four conditions must be satisfied. (1) There must be rules or principles valid for all individuals, not excluding God, rules definitive of individuality purely in general, or as a 'transcendental'. (2) There must be rules valid for all individuals *except* God, rules definitive of 'non-Divine individual', or of individuality as a secular or non-transcendental category. (3) There must be a criterion for the distinction between the two sets of rules. (4) There must be reasons why the distinction needs to be made.

The criterion in question derives from the definition of deity, which may be stated variously as 'worshipfulness', unsurpassability (by another), modal all-inclusiveness, or non-fragmentariness. These phrases I take to be equivalent.

False or at best ambiguous criteria, not equivalent to the foregoing, are: infinity, absoluteness, perfection or completeness, immutability, necessity, self-sufficiency or *aseity*, simplicity, uncaused cause, creator—if these are taken as excluding any and every application of their contraries to the divine reality.

Ordinary individuals, or individuals other than God, presumably in all possible cases, influence and are influenced by some but not all individuals. In other words individuals interact, they are both active and passive, causes and effects. However, with ordinary individuals the scope of interaction is fragmentary, less than cosmic. Also, the power of self-maintenance, or preservation of integrity through interaction, is ordinarily limited, and, therefore, the individual has not always existed; for, the conditions in which its self-maintenance is possible being limited, in infinite past time these conditions will not always have been provided. Any ordinary individual, since its scope of interaction and power of self-maintenance are limited, can conceivably be surpassed by another individual with greater scope and

power. Thus interaction that is surpassable in
scope and in power to maintain itself defines
ordinary individuality. Whatever is individual,
or one being, acts as one and responds as one
to actions of others; but, ordinarily, not everything is acted upon by the individual nor does
everything act upon it. Likewise its acting and
being acted upon have not always taken place
and will not always do so.

Since God, to be worshipful, must be unsurpassable, his scope cannot be less than cosmic, and there can be no possibility of an individual beyond the reach of his influence or
from which he could not receive influence.
Likewise, whereas ordinary individuals maintain themselves only in some environments,
not in all, the unsurpassable individual must
have unlimited ability to adapt to varying
states of reality. It is thus completely 'un-
specialized' in the ecological sense, possessing
an absolutely general or unsurpassable power
of adaptation to things. Hence there can be no
beginning or ending of its existence—one state
of affairs being neither more nor less suitable
for its existence than another—and thus the
notion of its nonexistence describes no positive state of affairs whatsoever, since it has no
ecological meaning. Only its existence has such
meaning. (This is one of the many forms of
the ontological proof.)

We now see how our four requirements may be met. (1) All individuals whatever interact. This is a strictly universal positive trait defining individuality as such. (2) All ordinary or non-divine individuals interact in surpassable, not unsurpassable, fashion, and hence they are generated and destroyed, partly ignorant of others and of themselves, and can adapt only more or less well to others. Combining (1) and (2), we deduce that 'divine individual' means an unsurpassably interacting being, hence without possible birth or death, incapable of poor or mediocre response to others— for instance, of complete or partial ignorance of self or others. (3) The criterion distinguishing the transcendental from the merely secular meaning of 'individual' is simply the distinction between the general idea of interaction as such, with scope and quality unspecified, and interaction definitely limited and surpassable, hence inappropriate to deity. In justification of the distinction, we may argue (4) that the idea of limited scope is intelligible only by contrast with that of unlimited or cosmic scope, and the idea of surpassability only by contrast with that of unsurpassability. Thus if secular individuality is conceivable so is divine individuality. This at least throws doubt on the positivist contention that theism is absurd. Moreover, as we shall see, a priori reasons can be given why individuals with restricted scope need to interact not only with one another but also with a being of unrestricted scope. Thus, without mentioning any truly empirical issues, we can see a rationale in theism which not only does no violence to any basic concept but is required by such concepts.

Classical theism is not in this position. It cannot use interaction, but only one-way action, as a transcendental. The idea of being acted upon, responding to influence, it must take as a category without transcendental application. But since the ground for contrasting ordinary or scope-limited action with transcendental or scope-unlimited action is no different from that for contrasting ordinary or scope-limited response with scope-unlimited response, to reject the second contrast is to deprive the first of any clear rationale. Nor can the rejection be justified religiously by invoking unsurpassability or worshipfulness. That a being with zero response must be better than one with ideal scope and power of response is far from self-evident. And the argument, 'If influence from another can do a being any good, the being must be defective or imperfect', begs the question, since perfection (in the sense that the argument requires), i.e., an all-around maximum of value, is no religious idea, and is logically problematic if not plainly absurd, and since a being cannot be termed surpassable merely because a verbal formula claims to describe its superior. We must know that the formula makes consistent sense. No such knowledge is available in the present case.

The conception of an ideal power of response has much better basis in ordinary categories than that of 'greatest possible actuality'. Concepts used to describe ordinary individuals do not need to be put in contrast with the supposed notion of a maximal possible value; whereas 'limited or fragmentary scope' does require its contrast with 'cosmic scope', and 'surpassable by another', its contrast with 'unsurpassable by another'.

Note that, as was pointed out in the previous chapter, if 'unsurpassable' meant 'absolutely, even by self', we should have the absurdity of a greatest possible reality. But to say that ordinary individuals can be surpassed both by self and others does not imply, as necessary contrasting concept, the notion of a simply unsurpassable individual, surpassable in no possible respect and neither by others nor by self. So long as we have the two concepts, surpassable and unsurpassable, we can perfectly well distinguish surpassability (or its negative) 'by self' from that 'by others', also surpassability 'in some respect' from that 'in all respects', and there is no logical reason to suppose that every grammatically permissible combination of these distinctions must make sense. Some combination of them must

make sense, but that is the only logical require-
ment. Classical theism seems to have selected
exactly that combination which fails to make
sense: i.e., 'in all respects unsurpassable even
by self'. But therewith possibility is taken as
absolutely maximizable. One could just as well
assume that 'greatest possible number' is a
definite conception.

To be fair one must see that the traditional
procedure had a certain plausibility. There is
indeed a profound and religiously relevant
asymmetry between acting and being acted
upon. Ordinary individuals are through and
through acted upon or caused, there is no independent individual trait in them, one which
was always able, or will always be able, to
maintain itself. Even their indispensable qualities are all caused. The extraordinary individual, in contrast, is acted upon or caused only
in its dispensable or contingent qualities, those
additional to its primordial-everlasting self-
identity as the sole unsurpassable being. This
unsurpassability itself is an abstract, yet truly
individual, form which is embodied anew in
concretely diverse ways in each divine state.
The form as such is not even self-surpassable.
God, one might say, is unsurpassably unsurpassable, and the adverb holds absolutely. Ordinary individuals have no such underived, unsurpassable, invulnerable form. They are sheer
effect; looking to the sufficiently remote past,

they have simply inherited "a world they never made," can never alter, and without which they would not have existed. But any world God inherits he also preceded and (with suitable qualifications) created. No one can influence God except someone already influenced by him. This statement would be absurd of any other being.

The asymmetry between the ordinary case of completely caused or dependent reality and only partly caused divine reality seems the chief reason why traditional theism could be found credible. If we abstract from God's contingent qualities, with respect to the rest of his reality we can view classical theism as largely correct. Here indeed is the uncaused cause, impassible, immutable, and all the rest of it. Only it is not God, nor—in spite of Thomism —is it an actuality, 'pure' or otherwise; rather, it is a mere abstraction from the contingent and caused actuality of the divine life. To identify God with this abstraction seems a philosophical species of idolatry. God is no such abstraction. He remains entirely free, in his full reality, to be receptive, enriched by his creatures, perpetually transcending himself, a genuinely active and loving subject, sympathetic companion of all existence. Eternally fixed, immune to influence, and incapable of increase is only the generic divine trait of universal interaction, unsurpassable in scope and adequacy

—just what is properly meant by calling God
'all-knowing', 'all-powerful', 'ubiquitous', also unborn and immortal. These abstractions
come to the same thing. But they are empty
by themselves. It is vain to interact universally
and always, but with nonentity, or to have unsurpassable knowledge, but of no other individual than self. But this emptiness is precisely
what classical theism spoke of as God when
it declared him absolutely and in all respects
immutable and independent of the world. If
love of the highest kind is ultimate, then so is
the social interdependence of which it is the
ideal form.

Now we are in a position to consider the
theistic proofs. The first is what I call the religious or 'global' proof (because in a fashion it sums up all the others). It is not
the usual argument from religious experience
taken as a mere fact. It is an argument from
the rational necessity of religious experience
and of God as its adequate referent. If an individual must have integrity in order to exist
as an individual, and if the conscious form of
integrity is worship, then while an individual
may live by unconscious integrity, or may to
some extent lack integrity, he cannot consciously and rationally choose to do either of
these. Hence there is something irrational in
choosing not to believe in God. There seems
no other way than the theistic to conceive the

objective correlate of personal integrity. How can various interests form one complex interest, various loves one complex love, unless the totality of objects of interest or love is felt to constitute a reality at least as unified or integrated as the creaturely individual? The whole of the previous chapter may be taken as the explication of this global reason for belief.

Some will urge against the foregoing that there can be no question of 'choosing', rationally or otherwise, to believe, for belief is either coerced by evidence or it is insincere. And even one who feels the need for worship may argue that it is wishful thinking to try to elicit evidence from a mere need.

I have two ways of countering this, either of which is to me personally almost convincing by itself.

The first way is to argue that the notion of wishful thinking is here inapplicable, the attempt to apply it deriving from an ambiguity in the notion of 'need' or 'wish'. Ordinary needs are matters of more or less. For some purposes, one needs this, for others, that, and the importance of the purposes is relative, not absolute. To be very happy a mother may need to believe that her son is not a criminal. Still if he is a criminal she may need and be able to face this fact in order to do her duty in the real world as it is. The very meaning of life does not depend, though it may almost seem to,

upon believing in the son's moral or legal innocence. The value of truth, closely connected
with ethical values, is not to be traded for the
value of dreams. But the wishfulness expressed
in such a trade is concerned with particular,
contingent, dispensable values. And they are
limited values, which can be outweighed by
others. On the contrary, the essential religious
value is not one value among others, it is not
measurable, contingent, or particular, but the
very principle of all achievement, really pre-
supposed by both the value of facing harsh
reality and the value of enjoying deceptive
dreams. If and only if life has meaning do
particular forms of life have meaning.

William James in his 'will to believe' failed
to make the above distinction with sufficient
clarity, and this was what spoiled his insight.
Where contingent alternatives, particular instances of value, are concerned, truth, 'facing
reality', has priority. Here it is absurd to argue,
"This view is good, the belief in it yields value,
hence we shall take it as true." For until we
know that it is factually true in some further
sense than that of giving satisfaction by being
believed we do not know what its value will
prove to be. 'True, therefore valuable', not
'valuable, therefore true', has to be the inference in all beliefs about contingent matters
—apart perhaps from suppositions about the
future which are scarcely beliefs but hopes or

states of confidence, as when we confidently jump over a crevasse. (Even here we have reasonable knowledge that something of the sort is possible.) No comforting illusion has right of way over acknowledgment of the real world in which all our obligations lie. But where an idea is so fundamental as to concern all possible contingent values, where a purpose is so basic as to be implicit in any reasonable or legitimate purpose, the pretence to reject the idea or purpose is itself a form of illusion. Any relative 'need' can be sacrificed in behalf of a relative need of greater dignity. But if there be an absolute 'need', one can sacrifice it only through confusion or inconsistency. There is something here deeper than a wish, or a merely contingent direction of will; rather, rational volition as such is in question. Hence the word 'need' is inadequate to describe it.

What I have been saying parallels rather closely Kant's contentions about the primacy of the practical will and also what Albert Schweitzer says in a similar vein. But there are differences. As will perhaps be already clear, my view as to why or how the idea of God is intrinsic to rational volition as such is dissimilar to Kant's, if not to Schweitzer's; and also I do not quite want to say that practical reason is primary in the drastic Kantian sense. It is, I think, decisive: that is, no one is foolish for taking its 'postulates' as definitive for him. The requirements of rational living cannot rationally be repudiated as mere illusions, since if all choice is irrational, so is the choice of rejecting illusion. But—and this is my second way of meeting the objection—the 'practical' argument is not primary in the radical sense of being the only decisive or cogent argument. The trouble with advocating the practical while rejecting all theoretical proofs, as Kant did, is that the impossibility of a theoretical argument for a conclusion would be no mean theoretical argument against it. If a belief is legitimate, evidence for it cannot be absolutely lacking. Nor can the evidence be merely moral. How can the moral side of our natures be so profound, if the theoretical side is so incurably superficial?

The global or religious argument is at best sadly compromised if we have to admit that it cannot be unpacked into more explicit arguments, at least some of them 'theoretical'. So let us consider these more explicit proofs. One of them argues (as we shall see in more detail presently) that localized interaction cannot of itself make intelligible the possibility of any order and that without some order the concept of interaction itself lacks definite meaning, so that the denial of a strictly universal yet individual form of interaction would be the denial of any interaction at all. And what sense could that have? This may be thought of as a form of the design argument for theism, which Thomas Aquinas more nearly correctly stated, in my judgment, than he did any of the others. (It was, as he stated it, rather far from the form of this argument which Kant refuted. Here, as at not a few points, Kant was a rather ignorant man, considering the almost unlimited scope of his ambitions and claims as a critic of natural theology.)

Again, since God alone is both contingent and necessary, whereas any other individual is simply contingent, or dispensable, a theistic proof might consist in showing that purely contingent existence is not self-sufficient or intelligible by itself, so that to deny God would be, absurdly enough, to reject any and every form of existence. (As I have argued elsewhere, that something exists is no mere fact, but an a priori truth.) This is the cosmological argument.

Moreover, since God's existence has an aspect of necessity, something like an ontological proof must be possible. The multitudinous opponents of this proof do chiefly two things: first, they take advantage of a bad mistake made by Anselm, repeated by Descartes, but —as some of us think we have shown—inessential to the ontological proof as such; second, they appeal to an alleged axiom that all existence, existence as such, must be logically contingent. But to put God under this rule is no more legitimate than to put him under the rule that individuals interact locally rather than cosmically, or are more or less ignorant. As we have seen, if all otherwise universal rules must apply also to God the word God stands for nonsense. This positivistic position can be defended, but if that is the ground upon which Anselm's proof is being attacked, let the critics state as much and stop confusing the issue. God's existence could not, logically could not, be merely contingent. Perhaps God could not exist at all, the idea being absurd, but that he should exist contingently is then doubly absurd. This much of the Anselmian position is, or ought to be, truistic; and it is time this was taught in elementary philosophy classes, instead of being incompetently 'refuted' by virtue of an axiom which simply begs the question and makes nonsense of the religious idea.

But note that, on the view I am defending, God is both necessary and contingent and that this combination, not necessity alone, is his uniqueness. It is analytic that no a priori proof for a contingent actuality, divine or not, could make sense. And this seems to be the intuitive ground for the stubborn opposition to an ontological proof. Such a proof could not give us God as a concrete actuality. The concrete divinity can only be contingent and empirical. Thus the particular actual world which presents itself to the divine experience, hence the particular character of the divine experience itself as receptive of the world, is knowable, if at all, empirically only. For instance, God as the God of humanity is but an empirical fact; for there might have been no humanity. A priori is only the "God of whatever creatures there are." Anselm and Descartes quite missed the logical significance of this obvious distinction. Their opponents missed it no less, though somewhat differently. The popular combination, through the centuries, of the two incompatible propositions: God is wholly uncaused or necessary, but our evidence for him, if any, must be wholly empirical, is a logical scandal. At least one of these propositions must be false or absurd. Are not both absurd? God must be necessary and contingent, and our knowledge of him must have an a priori and also an empirical aspect.

The empirical aspect of God, however, concerns, not his existence or eternal character, but only the accidental or generated qualities constituting, with the eternal aspect, his full reality. The bare question of the divine existence is purely nonempirical. Hence empirical existential proofs in natural theology are bound to be fallacious. Here I agree entirely with Hume and Kant.

Does it follow that the ontological proof alone holds? No, for it is distinguished from others not by being a priori, nor by arguing from concepts, but rather by taking as its premise the intelligibility of one concept, that of

deity, or Worshipfulness. Other equally a priori
arguments can be based on concepts not initially identified with this. Thus, in the reasonable argument from design, we may argue that
if all interaction is supposed to be local and
more or less unknowing, it is not to be understood how reality could be or remain anything
but a "shapeless chaos"—to quote Jefferson's
phrase, used in this connection. Only universal
interaction can secure universal order, or im-
pose and maintain laws of nature cosmic in
scope and relevant to the past history of the
universe. This argument is not observational.
For, if the reasoning is correct, the alternative
to God's existence is not an existing chaos
but, rather, nothing conceivable. The argument
is that the very concept of reality (and any
significant 'unreality' as well) implicitly in-
volves order and an orderer. Apart from God
not only would this world not be conceivable,
but no world, and no state of reality, or even
of unreality, could be understood. It is not any
mere fact that must be rejected—according to
a properly conceived natural theology—if theism is rejected, but the basic concepts by which
alone we can conceive even possible facts. All
the arguments are just as truly a priori as the
ontological.

One may, for instance, argue from such basic
concepts as truth, beauty, or goodness. These,
taken in their ultimate generality, are not em-

pirical ideas. It is not just our human values, or terrestrial animal values, but any values for any possible valuer, which require divine valuations to make sense. Thus consider goodness. A rational ethics requires what Kant termed the *summum bonum,* or the supreme rational aim for any rational being as such. This is an a priori conception (one which could be formulated in any world in which philosophizing could go on). But Kant misconceived the content of the rational aim. He said we should hope to combine complete virtue with complete happiness, this combination to be our individual possession approximated to in some infinite post-terrestrial state. But absolutes like perfect happiness combined with perfect virtue, so far as they make sense at all, are divine prerogatives. It is God's combination of these qualities, not ours, which alone can furnish the aim of all effort. True, our efforts must be able to aid the divine self-realization, and this would have seemed impossible to Kant since he held the Aristotelian dogma that God must be without receptivity, immune to possible influence from the creatures. According to our previous discussion, however, this denial of divine reaction or interaction is mistaken. Once it has been renounced, the way is open to reconceive the *summum bonum* as the divine life itself, to which all creatures in their measure contribute. Serving God is then truly the inclusive aim. To this aim no creature is irrelevant. Not that we help God to be virtuous—this would indeed be absurd. But we may contribute to the richness of his 'happiness', the beauty of the contents of his always perfectly righteous experience.

Our ancestors were afflicted with a subtle egoism. They wanted to serve God everlastingly, but with the understanding that he also would serve them everlastingly. A fair bargain, as it were! However, since their logic was confused enough to permit them at the same time to deny divine receptivity, they were really saying that while God would everlastingly serve them, they could do nothing for him, since he is immune to gifts, or to being enhanced or influenced in any way, an absolute marvel of self-sufficiency and indifference. So, in effect, God serves his creatures forever; they do not, in any intelligible sense, serve him. He is the means to our achievement, we are neither means nor end for him—but, in value terms, bare nothing. My proposal is that we should serve God for our time, rather than forever, and should trust him in a suitable sense to serve us also for our time.

Only in one sense do we serve God forever. Since He, having unsurpassable memory, cannot lose what he has once acquired, in acquiring us as we are on earth he acquires us forevermore. But we do not in the same sense acquire him forevermore. (Whether we like it or not, there are divine prerogatives which cannot be ours.) Personally I find this by no means basically sad or troublesome. Though we do not forever continue to serve God, our temporary service is everlasting in a sense which I find deeply satisfying: whatever enters the treasury of the divine life is at once where moths cannot corrupt and thieves cannot break through nor steal. And we can in this life be aware of ourselves as already immortal elements in deity, and so by Love we participate now in our immortality. The triumph over death as our triumph is now, not in a magical future. But apart from God, is not the triumph with death?

Is this an empirical argument? No, any possible thinking creatures, in no matter what state of reality, would face the essential problem. Rationality as such requires that there be an aim which it is rational to pursue in spite of the mortality of nondivine individuals and species of individuals. But only deity provides a clear meaning for immortality. And only an all-loving deity whom all may love can provide nondivine individuals, even though vicariously, with permanent achievement for their effort. This is so, not because of contingent features of our world, but because in any world God alone could and would be universally loving, universally lovable, and everlasting.

Nontheistic substitutes for a divine orderer and a divine immortalizer of achievements seem but makeshifts. 'Matter' is just a label for the orderly processes of nature, it is not a positive principle to explain their possibility. The old notion that "in infinite time atoms would by chance fall into all possible arrangements" was a naive begging of the question. To talk of this or that set of atoms is to talk of a kind of order, not to explain that kind. The mere existence of atoms with definite character, maintaining themselves through time and relative to one another, is already a tremendous order. Materialism in principle refuses to take order as a problem.

Again, the purely humanistic version of immortality, 'social immortality', is an evasion. Our contributions to human life do, to some small extent, survive our death; but to suppose mere humanity capable of preserving even this partial contribution strictly forever is to blur the distinction between the known traits of humanity and the idea of God in a fashion which I at least find wildly irrational. The other alternative, living only for the finite, vaguely foreseeable but limited human future, seems also irrational. It is animal instinct which we then fall back upon to give us a sense of life's value; it is not our philosophy or religion. I am fond of the subhuman animals, but I think we should accept our human role of living in the light of conscious aims.

Let us consider the classical objections to the argument for a divine orderer. First, the argument was generally stated as proceeding from the premise that the actual empirically-given order and detailed pattern of the world is too good and beautiful to be thought less than a divine product. The objectors promptly (in the time of Carneades, for example) pointed to what, for our human judgment, cannot but appear as flaws in the world picture. A partially botched product can hardly be sufficient evidence for a perfect producer. Both parties, I hold, were mistaken. Any world would require a divine orderer, and therefore the contingent characters of this world are irrelevant, one way or the other. All that these characters can do is to throw light on the contingent qualities, additional to his existence, which God may have. Furthermore, unsurpassably universal knowledge and love are not among the contingent, rather they belong to the necessary or definitional, characters of deity. To the question, Why then the partial disorder and evils in the world? a creationist philosophy has essentially but one answer. It holds that it is not God alone who acts in the world; every individual acts. There is no single producer of the actual series of events; one producer, to be sure, is uniquely universal, unsurpassably influential.

Nevertheless, what happens is in no case the product of his creative acts alone. Countless choices, including the universally influential choices, intersect to make a world, and how, concretely, they intersect is not chosen by anyone, nor could it be. A multiplicity of choosers means that what concretely happens is never simply chosen; rather, it just happens. Purpose, in multiple form, and chance are not mutually exclusive but complementary; neither makes sense alone. ('Purpose not in multiple form' is, I believe, contradictory or mere gibberish.) Concrete evils and goods simply happen, they are never in their full particularity chosen. Hence to ask, Why did God choose to inflict this or that evil upon us? is to ask a pseudo-question.

The order of the world requires a divine orderer, not because the order is perfect, or because there is nothing chaotic or unfortunate in the series of events, but because apart from God there is no way to understand how there could be any limits at all to the confusion and anarchy implied by the notion of a multiplicity of creative agents, none universally influential or wise. And that there are such limits to anarchy is no mere fact; for there would have to be limits in any genuinely conceivable state of reality. But to understand this necessity is to see it as one with the necessary existence of God as cosmic orderer.

A second trouble with the classical proof from order was that God's ordering was supposed to be done in eternity, entirely uninfluenced by any creaturely decisions. Indeed, the creaturely decisions were themselves divinely chosen. But then the divine cause of all things was a sheer exception to the rule that concrete effects are also concrete causes, and vice versa, and also to the rule that the cause precedes, the effect follows. To say that one individual is merely cause, not effect, is to say that it is merely prior to others. But God outlasts us as definitely as he precedes us; there is no logic in making him cause only, and not also effect. On the neoclassical view, as I call it, God is both before and after, both cause and effect, of all events.

What then is left of the customary objection that theism must misuse the concept of cause? True, the bare existence of God is no effect and is prior to everything rather than subsequent to everything. But this strictly prior existence is not God as concrete cause of anything; it is God conceived abstractly in his bare self-identity, not his full contingent actuality. As *concrete* cause of each event, God is always also effect of prior events, including prior divine events or experiences. Thus we admit a rule applicable to all causes, even divine. That God, and only God, can also be abstract cause in so extreme a sense that, in this aspect, he is

not effect at all is an obvious logical consequence of his being the universal individual,
confined to no one stretch of space-time, the
very principle of reality as such. But in this universal role, deity is abstract, a mere outline of
reality. The concrete is always more than any
universal, it is always an instance of universals.
Each concrete divine state is an instance of the
transcendental, 'concrete actuality', and of the
divine attribute, unsurpassability. (For not even
God could surpass his response to the same
actual state of the world.)

A third objection to the design argument is
that it does not exclude polytheism. But (a) the
point of the argument is that only strictly universal and unsurpassable interaction can explain cosmic order, and (b) to assign two or
more individuals the role of universal interactor is to imply a distinction without a
difference, or utter confusion. Each cosmic
interactor would have to interact with the
others, and then there would be no overall
integrity, and one might as well have no cosmic
interactor. Order is in principle 'the rule of
one'. Even a committee needs a chairman, and
not two chairmen but one. (To posit several
not quite universal interactors is a notion which
throws no light at all on any problem. For one
thing, the status of being nearly universal, even
if supposed by chance to obtain at a given

moment, must be inherently unstable to an unlimited degree.)

In a sense, however, the objection points to
a truth, the old Platonic one that evil and
partial disorder in the world do mean more
than one agent influencing reality. However,
there is no clear sense in which this can amount
to a plurality of 'gods'. One (there is no room
for more) unsurpassable or divine agent, with
a multiplicity of surpassable ones, covers both
the possibility of order and that of partial
disorder.

When Kierkegaard said that 'God' was "not
a name but a concept" he stated a half truth,
just as did Tillich when he said that God was
not a being but being itself. For, in this unique
case, a word is both name of an individual and
label for a universal property (unsurpassability). To say that this cannot be is to say that
God cannot be. And more than ordinary gram-
mar is required to establish that! This case is
linguistically unique, just as God is existen-
tially unique. To the charge that one commits
a category mistake in regarding a certain property as self-individuated, the countercharge is
in order: since nothing can be worshipfully
superior to all and at the same time simply
one more instance under ordinary categorial
rules applied in the ordinary way, it is the
objector who misapplies categories. In the old
language, 'God' does not connote a class.

Without doubt someone in this controversy is misusing concepts, but (*pace* Gilbert Ryle) it is just the question at issue over again which side is doing this.

Is it a rule without possible exception that all individuals are surpassable? Then theism is absurd, as positivism says it is. Is the rule subject to a possible but not necessary exception? This will not do, for a nonnecessary being is *ipso facto* surpassable. Is the rule subject to a necessary though unique exception? Then theism is necessarily true. In support of this, consider the following: the exceptional status of God can itself be put as a transcendental or strictly universal rule. Thus, "Every individual whatsoever interacts (at least) with *some* other individuals, and also, and *in all possible cases,* with God, who alone universally interacts." This rule is absolute. For since God, in a fashion, interacts with, that is, both influences and (in subsequent states) is influenced by, himself, all individuals whatever interact with deity, as well as with at least some individuals other than deity.

It is also to be noted that all the exceptional properties essential to deity are in themselves universal rules of a kind, under which innumerable instances can come. Thus of *any* divine state the rule holds that it accomplishes a not conceivably surpassable synthesis of its actual data. And the number of possible, perhaps also of actual, divine states is more than finite.

We thus have three sorts of rules: (1) those definitive of individuals other than divine, that is, of surpassable, not universally interacting, localized or fragmentary individuals; (2) those definitive of all individuals whatever, individuality purely as such; finally (3) rules definitive of the unsurpassable individual. And we have intelligible relations between these three kinds of rules. What more could one ask for? If this is not a rational view, what would be?

If local interaction requires cosmic interaction to set limits to chaos and mutual frustration, does not cosmic interaction require local interaction, as a ruler requires citizens to rule? Also, a multiplicity of ephemeral purposive agents requires a single everlasting agent whose purposes embrace the whole and give permanence to the values of the parts. But without parts there is also no whole. Thus 'God as such' and 'creature as such' have each its a priori status and function, and these are complementary. But this symmetry is embraced in a profound asymmetry. *God as such* is individual, while *creature as such* is an extremely general class. Only the nonemptiness of the class is necessary or a priori, not the individual members of the class. God requires *a* world, but not *the* world. By contrast, what the world requires is not simply *a* God but *the* one and only possible God, the Worshipful One. Thus God in his eternal necessity is alone and unrivalled among individuals.

CHAPTER THREE

Why There Cannot be Empirical Proofs

The collapse of natural or rational theology in the eighteenth century had a number of causes, some of which have been touched on. Perhaps the most important of all was an inappropriate definition of deity, inappropriate not only because it failed to express the meaning of worship, the intuitive ground of the idea of God, but also because it involved the philosophically baseless supposition that 'greatest possible actuality' makes sense and because it resulted in antinomies from which two millennia failed to find an issue, so long as the definition was retained, but which disappear when it is given up.

Another cause of the 'collapse' was the supposed distinction between the 'a priori' onto-

logical argument and the 'a posteriori' cosmological and design arguments. This is an unclear
and essentially erroneous distinction. On the
one hand, all those who accepted the ontological argument held that among the implications of the reasoning was the view that in
thinking God we in a fashion also experience
him, so that the argument, though a priori, is
also in a sense experiential. On the other hand,
the cosmological and design arguments are not
really 'empirical' in the sharp sense which
goes beyond 'experiential' as just used. This
sharp sense is the one that Popper first clearly
defined: that is empirical in the distinctive
sense which some conceivable experience
would falsify. It is not enough that experience
can illustrate or confirm a proposition; if it is
to be usefully called empirical, experience must
conceivably be able to disconfirm it. But what
advocate of 'empirical arguments' for theism
(Tennant? Brightman?) has told us how experience might conceivably show that God did *not*
exist? Did Thomas, advocate of the 'a posteriori' method, do this? I think not. I hold that
this test is decisive. On the one hand, God,
being ubiquitous, can be experienced, but then
all sorts of things, including the relations of
numbers in finite arithmetic, can be experienced, no matter how a priori in the logical
sense. But on the other hand, God, being the
sole necessarily existing individual, could not

possibly be disconfirmed by a contingent fact;
and so in the useful or distinctive sense his
existence is not 'empirical'.

Let us see how this nonempirical status results from our treatment of individuals as subject to the universal rule that they all interact with at least some other individuals. To say,
'with some' is to prompt the query: with how
many, and which ones? The answer cannot
be given a priori: one must point in the per-
ceived world to the particular individuals. But
'all the individuals which there are, without
possible exception', is definite a priori. True,
we do not know a priori which individuals
actually fill the role of interacting with God,
but we do not need to know this in order to
have defined just the one divine individual. For
he alone could in any world have unrestricted
scope of interaction. No further principle of
individuation is needed or possible. Whereas
the role of local interaction simply as such is
highly indefinite and specifies no one individual, the role of universal interaction is unique.

The only other unique case specifiable a priori is that of zero interaction. According to
this, God may act, but cannot be acted upon.
Classical theism chose this zero case as definitive of deity. The choice was doubly blind, in
that the universal case was ignored, rather
than carefully scrutinized on its merits, and in
that no attention was paid to the apparent im-

possibility of making sense out of an acting agent which cannot *inter*act, or of an individual which cannot relate itself to other individuals. There was even a third oversight, the fact that religious language is full of implications of interaction between God and his creatures. And since the universal form of interaction is just as truly unique a priori as the supposed zero form, nothing is lost by choosing it instead, while much is gained.

If the individuality of God could be specified empirically only, the existence of God could be no more than an empirical or contingent fact. God would then be a mere creature, something which might never have existed, rather than the uncreated creator, presupposition of existence and nonexistence, itself without presupposition. Our ancestors realized this necessity that God's essential uniqueness be purely conceptual, hence a priori, not factual. But they failed to analyze and generalize sufficiently the problems involved. To say, as they did, that God is conceptually unique because he alone does *not* react or interact is only a negative description. Negation is parasitic on affirmation. In God himself, at least, his uniqueness must be positive. But the sole possible positive correlative to 'absolute', 'independent', or 'uncaused' is 'relative', 'dependent' or 'caused'; and if God is in no way effect, then his relation to the world must be as

mere or uncaused cause. And since universal
scope of relativity, or of being effect, is just as
a priori as zero scope, but has the advantage
over the latter of enabling us to preserve the
well-founded rule that to be an individual power
is to interact, we have excellent ground for
taking universal interaction to be the positive
feature in the divine mode of action.

Another consequence of this choice is that
the divine 'absoluteness' becomes genuinely
explanatory of relative existence, instead of being merely opposed to it. The divine interaction is strictly or 'absolutely' universal.
However, the concrete content of this absolute
universality must be relative, varying with
the actual world. God interacts with whatever
individuals there are, but what individuals are
there? This is the contingent, relative, or
empirical aspect, yet it is integral to the concrete realization of the absolute aspect. One
cannot interact except with existing individuals. But one could, it seems, be *without* interaction, even were there no other individuals.
Thus the negative theology makes creation
an irrelevant excrescence. The divine absoluteness, neoclassically conceived, is a relative
absoluteness, it is universality, on the one hand
specified a priori and obtaining by necessity,
but on the other hand always existing concretely
with respect to some actual contingent world.
All the individuals there are God interacts with,

but not all individuals there might be; for one cannot interact with the nonexistent.

Here we see what was wrong with the classical, and Kantian, idea of 'most real being'. This was a definition, not with respect to actuality, but with respect to possibilities only. All the value or reality there could be, that God was said to have, no matter what the world might be. But therewith the contrast between actual and possible is hopelessly compromised, and the meaning of both terms is put in doubt. Worse, if possible, our struggle to realize possible values in the world becomes a mere absurdity or impertinence. Act as we may, perfection, all possible value, just is actual if classical theism is correct. It is odd that a theory should demonstrate the absolute irrelevance of the theorizing agent and his achievements.

Instead of ascribing to the Unsurpassable the actualization of all possible perfection, we should ascribe to him the actual possession only of all in fact actualized values. The entire actual world is his to enjoy in all-embracing vision. We should further ascribe to him the potential possession of every possible value. Were such and such a possible value actual for anyone, it would *a fortiori* be actual for God, who would enjoy unsurpassable knowledge of it. For no mode of possession of value is more absolute than full awareness. Once more we

find that unrestricted scope, relative to the
actual world, but specified a priori and obtaining by primordial necessity, gives us what we
need. The divine actuality is logically coextensive with all actuality and, in this sense, is actuality itself; the divine potentiality is coextensive
with all possibility and is possibility itself. Any
actual thing God enjoys actually; any possible thing would be his actual possession were
it actual for anyone. From this 'modal coincidence' it follows that though God can increase
in value, he can be surpassed by no other than
himself. For any increase anywhere is *a fortiori*
increase in him. He grows, but his mode of
growth, as Fechner sagaciously said long ago,
is incomparably superior to all other modes.
Or, as he put it "the perfection of God is his
ideal mode of perfectibility." If he surpasses
himself, it is in an unsurpassable manner.

One reason why this solution of the problem
of perfection was so generally and so long
overlooked was that it is a rather natural verbal
confusion to suppose that the unsurpassable
cognitive power must survey all possible as
well as all actual values, and since to know a
value is, as I have just stated, to possess it, it
may seem that the actualization of a possible
value gives God's knowledge no quality it
would otherwise lack. Thus if a merely possible valuable quality Q is known to God, he
possesses Q no less than if it were actualized.

This is the paradox inherent in the verbal expression, 'possible world'. If possibilities have, item for item, all the qualities of the corresponding actualities, then actualization is meaningless and indeed adds no value. But this should teach us that possibilities are not to be viewed as qualitatively identical with actualities, apart from some quality-free factor of actualization. Actualization must somehow be qualitative enhancement, or the concept is vacuous.

The solution to the riddle is to see that merely possible qualities are lacking in individual definiteness. There are no possible individuals, but only possible kinds of individuals, possibilities for further individuation. As Peirce insisted, possibility is in principle general rather than particular, determinable rather than determinate. It is in some degree indefinite, and so, since value lies in harmonized contrasts and the more definite a thing is the richer the contrasts it can involve, it follows that possible worlds, really worldly possibilities or incompletely definite sorts of worlds, are less rich as objects of knowledge than actual worlds. Thus God does not possess actually all possible value simply by knowing all possibilities.

Since actualization is determination, and "all determination is [partial] negation," as Spinoza said, actuality as such is finite, and only mere possibility can be strictly infinite. The 'absolutely infinite' cannot be determinate; so far from being the fulfillment of all possible richness or plenitude of reality, it is the fulfillment of *no* possible value. It is the ultimate determinable, abstracting from any and every actual determination, by itself wholly indefinite, and thus empty of contrast and devoid of beauty. Actualization is the acceptance of limitation; it requires choice among incompatible values, this and therefore not that, or that and therefore not this. (I wonder what great philosopher before Whitehead clearly stated this, and systematically drew the consequences?) God in creating worlds faces such a choice, also. Even for him, to do all possible things is to do nothing. But worship does not require sheer infinity—a formless emptiness at best—taken as actual. It requires that God's potentiality, what he could be, must be as wide as the absolute infinity of logically possible values. That is, no value can be possible in itself, yet impossible for God.

To worship the infinity of God's power, what he is capable of being, as though it were simply the same as his actuality is idolatry, so far as I can see. And it implies the sheer irrelevance of all creaturely choices. God is not on one side only of categorial contrasts; he is not merely infinite or merely finite, merely absolute or merely relative, merely cause or merely effect, merely agent or merely patient, merely actual or merely potential, but in all cases both, each in suitable respects or aspects of his living reality, and in such a manner as to make him unsurpassable by another. He is even both joy and sorrow, both happiness and sympathetic participation in our griefs. He is not indeed both goodness and wickedness, but only because the latter is a privation, disregard of the interests of others, and this, like 'ignorance of what is', conflicts with 'unsurpassable by another'. But loving participation in grief, like receptivity to influence in general, is no privation, but a positive power, extremely limited in us, unlimited in God.

Neoclassical theism can say and mean, "God is love." The unsurpassable could not be without love—for even we ourselves would surpass a loveless being. To love is to rejoice with the joys and sorrow with the sorrows of others. Thus it is to be influenced by those who are loved. An entity may be influenced by all, by some, or by no other entities—these are the three cases specifiable a priori. Examples fitting the third or zero case are not hard to find, for abstractions, just so far as they are abstract, are immune to influence. What can one do to change the number two? Also, past events are henceforth immune to influence. Deceased individuals are indeed 'impassible'. But living individuals . . .? It seems that contemporary individuality is recognizable only through interaction. So there are basically just two possibilities, an individual interacting 'with some', or 'with all'.

Let us sum up our discussion so far. If for ordinary existence there cannot be conceptual proofs but only empirical or factual evidence, this is because ordinary individuals cannot be defined by concepts alone; if for divine existence, on the contrary, there cannot be empirical evidence but can be conceptual evidence, this is because divine individuality is defined purely conceptually. Not only does the divine existence not conflict with any truly necessary conceptual rule, it is even the sole individual existence which expresses such a rule. The other individuals are just facts, permitted but not called for by any rational reason.

Kant said that "concepts without percepts are empty," true enough; but the bare existence or individuality of God is indeed empty, the mere universal divine outline of existence without concrete or particular content. Kant's error was in supposing that the existence of an individual is its entire actuality. Not so; that John Smith, born and baptized forty years ago, still exists leaves unspecified all the concrete details of his actual history since birth. Analogously, that God, never born at all, still exists, always has existed, and always must exist leaves unspecified an unimaginable fullness of particular actuality. Mere 'existing deity', without further information, is indeed in a sense an empty concept. However—it is a concept formally incapable of lacking actualization. It can be actualized in an infinity of alternative ways, but unactualized it cannot be. So the empty conceptual knowledge that God exists does tell us that his individuality is actualized *somehow*. How it is actualized is for science, revelation, personal experience, some form of empirical knowledge, to tell us, so far as we can know it at all. This of course is not very far. Our knowledge of the concrete divine reality is negligibly small.

There is mystery enough about God, not because his eternal 'essence' is inaccessible, or because metaphysics or natural theology is moonshine or impossible, but because particular actuality, even divine actuality, is not metaphysical but empirical. Perception, human or divine, is the only avenue to particular actuality. But in one unique case, it is not the avenue to existence or individual identity. Rather, conceptual, or if you prefer, spiritual, insight is this avenue, for the reason that this individuality is specifiable only a priori or nonsensuously. Whereas empirically individuated entities must exist, if at all, empirically, the entity individuated a priori cannot exist empirically.

The rules for individuality as such permit but do not require any one particular individual with localized scope of interaction; but they could not even permit, unless they also required, the individual with universal scope. This scope presupposes only the meaning of the rules for its uniqueness, whereas 'not universal' is infinitely far from unique. To say that the rules for individuality are neutral to the divine existence is to talk confusedly, since it takes two parties to make a harmony, and the idea of God, or of worship, does not allow the rules to be neutral. They must either be hostile to worship a priori, in which case worship is a kind of nonsense, or else favorable a priori, in which case both atheism and positivism, along with empirical theism, are in some fashion nonsensical. Either everything (in some degree) serves God—everything actual actually, everything possible potentially—or nothing serves or could serve him, and the idea is empty of coherent meaning. Either God is lord over possibility as well as actuality, or he is bare nothing, mere conceptual confusion. All other kinds of individuals are thought of as controlling some actualities or some possibilities; accordingly, they may or may not exist. This will not do for God, who is all or nothing, inherent in any fact, affirmed in any affirmation, any possible hypothesis, or in none.

Still otherwise, 'God' is not simply another word in our language but, if anything rational, a name for the principle back of every word in any possible language. He is not merely another topic to think about, but the all-pervasive medium of knowledge and things known, to recognize whom is a way of thinking about no matter what. The question remains, is it a significant, coherent way of thinking about no matter what? That alone is the question.

If the central issue of natural theology were a scientific one, it would be conceivable that observational or contingent facts might justify a negative decision. But any god with whom facts could conflict is an idol, a fetish, correlative to idolatry, not to genuine worship. Divinity being all actuality in one individual actuality, and all possibility in one individual potentiality or capacity for actuality, a possible divine nonexistence, must, like any other possible reality, be a possible state of God and content of some possible divine knowledge. But a being could not, logically could not, know itself as never having existed. Nor could a divine being know itself, as we know ourselves, as having come into existence after previously not existing. Thus to treat the existential question of natural theology as scientific or factual is to change the subject from the question of the reality of a being whose interaction is strictly universal to that of one whose scope of interaction is in principle limited. But if not all possible values belong even potentially to God, what could prevent a conceivable rival from surpassing him by actualizing these values? And can a being open to rivalry be worshipped in the strict or exalted sense?

To ask, as the empirical theist or atheist does, "Is the world such that it must have been, or could have been, divinely created?" implies two kinds of possible worlds, the one kind requiring (or at least permitting?) a Creator, and the other not. What would distinguish the two kinds? Is it the proportion of good to evil? But at what point in the continuum between more and less evil would a possible world abruptly become compatible with being divinely created? Or is it a question of greater and greater probability of such createdness? Does any of this make sense? I am not joking, for I seriously believe that the empiricist program is at this point nonsensical.

We are told by an English writer that it is a question of whether there be any 'utterly senseless' or 'unredeemed' evil? What would such a thing be like? I declare in all earnestness I have no idea. Any evil has some value from some perspective, for even to know it exists is to make it contributory to a good, knowledge itself being a good. But any evil is also in some degree a misfortune, and in my opinion the theological 'problem of evil' is quite miscon-

ceived if it is seen as that of justifying particular
evils. Evils are to be avoided where possible;
where not, to be mitigated or utilized for good
in whatever way possible—but never, for
heaven's sake never, to be metaphysically
justified. The voice from the whirlwind in the
Book of Job says not one word about evil
being good in disguise or not really evil after
all, and theologians might perhaps learn from
this illustrious example. The justification of evil
is not that it is really good or partly good or
necessary to good, but that the creaturely freedom from which evils spring, with probability
in particular cases and inevitability in the general case, is also an essential aspect of all
goods, so that the price of a guaranteed absence
of evil would be the equally guaranteed absence
of good. Thus not even the nastiest or most
conceivably unhelpful evil could have anything
to do with the nonexistence of God. Risk of
evil and opportunity for good are two aspects
of just one thing, multiple freedom; and that
one thing is also the ground of all meaning
and all existence. This is the sole, but sufficient,
reason for evil as such and in general, while
as for particular evils, by definition they have
no ultimate reason. They are nonrational.

It is argued that a divinely-created world
must absolutely lack evil, be devoid of suffering
and frustration, as well as of wicked intentions.
But could 'good' mean anything in a world

in which any contrasting term would be totally excluded by omnipotent power? And in such a world how could the creatures, who would have no genuine options, even know what was meant by divine freedom to choose this world out of the totality of possibilities? And if they could not know it, then the envisaged perfect world would be one in which at least the good of creaturely understanding of the creator was quite impossible. Or, if there is not to be even divine choice among possibilities, then God would not be responsible in an ethical sense for good or evil; indeed, he would not be subject to ethical criteria, and hence evils would cease to be relevant as disproofs of his perfection, which is in effect being conceived as having nothing to do with ethics, one way or another.

For creationist or neoclassical metaphysics deity must be the supreme or unsurpassable form of creative freedom. But 'supreme' or 'unsurpassable' form cannot be the only possible form. In creationist metaphysics, all concrete reality is in principle creative. But then what happens is never, as it stands, simply attributable to 'the' creator, but only to deity *and* the creatures together. Reality is always in part self-created, *causa sui*, creativity being, in this philosophy, the supreme transcendental. All creatures have creativity above zero, all are creators.

If the evils of the world are not an empirical disproof of deity, what more likely negative evidence could there be? I see no plausible candidate. The 'degradation of energy'? Only if the principle were known to be the last word from a cosmic and everlasting perspective, and this, I take it, utterly exceeds any possible observational insight. Only omniscience itself could know this. And omniscience could also alter it, or could know it as its own free decision, and as compatible with its own unsurpassable goodness.

There is one last stand for the empiricist to make: the existence of any world at all is what proves God. So, then, were there nothing worldly, there would also be nothing superworldly or divine? What then would there be— just bare nothing, not anything? And what does this mean? I note the words, but for me they do not add up to a definite and coherent meaning. 'There would not be anything'—what do 'there' and 'be' stand for in this context? There are lions because, somewhere, it is true that *'there* is a lion'. But 'there' gets its meaning from things, not from sheer emptiness. 'There' means, in the neighborhood of, or in a certain direction and at a certain distance from, the speaker or the hearer. But with 'there is not anything', even 'there is' seems to lose all definiteness. In addition, if I am right that God's unsurpassability implies that his potentiality is coincident with possibility itself, even the 'possibility of nothing' must express something which God could be or have. But universal nonexistence, including his own, he logically could not be or have. It follows that the possibility of 'nothing worldly', if indeed it be a possibility, cannot imply the possibility of divine nonexistence, but only of God existing in solitude. In that case, it is silly to argue, 'Deity exists because there is a creature'. For either God is incapable of sheer idleness, of not creating, in which case it is no contingent fact that there is something creaturely but an a priori necessity; or, if he is capable of sheer idleness, then he can and would exist even were there not anything worldly. Take it either way, his existence depends upon no empirical fact.

Of course, our being able to know the divine existence depends upon the empirical fact of our existence. But to say, 'we exist, therefore we know God exists' is ambiguous. If it means that only the existent can know, it is correct. If, however, it means that our evidence that God exists is that we exist, it is illogical. The difference between our existing and our not existing can have nothing to do with a difference between God's existing and his not existing. And this remains true even if we generalize from ourselves to worldly existence in general or as such. For, once more, if God could not exist without some world or other, this would only imply that with his unsurpassable creativity he infallibly provides himself with a world; and then it is no mere fact that there is one. And if (which I question) he could exist without a world, it is illogical to say, 'Because there is a world God must exist'. In no case can a sheer necessity obtain because one contingent alternative rather than another is realized. The precritical Kant saw and said this clearly, but in the heat of his critical arguments he partly lost sight of its importance.

The search for an empirical meaning for the existential question about God has failed. If this is what Tillich wants to say by the rather violent method of refusing to admit the word existence in relation to God, "more power to him." Hume and Kant actually understated the case against empirical proofs; the entire attempt was ludicrously inept. It is a conceptual question, a question of self-understanding, clarity, and consistency.

I know by experience how mightily men will struggle against the foregoing argument. They will say, yes *if* there is a God, then all possibility is his potentiality, but only if. But (a) there is an 'if' only where there is a contrary possibility; and (b) the possibility of a Godless world is the possibility of something which God *could not* (logically could not) know, were it actual. And thus his power to know is being conceived as subject to limitation, and then I can conceive a superior individual with unlimited power to know, and what you have been calling God is therewith exhibited as only an idol. Suppose God to exist (if this is inconceivable, then indeed our issue is not one of fact but of meaning), yet to exist so that his nonexistence would have been possible, or remains a conceivable alternative. Then God must, so to speak, say to himself, "There is something which conceivably might have been, but which I could not conceivably have known." Is this the conception of God, or of an idol? It seems to me that it is the latter. We need not and should not define God as 'all possible perfections'; for there are incompossible value possibilities, and so the phrase is nonsense. But we should define him as the all-inclusive yet individual actuality, and the all-inclusive yet individual potentiality. And then all—simply all—questions of fact take the form, 'Which among divine potentialities are actualized?' None can take the form, 'Are any divine potentialities actualized?' For that implies the meaningless notion of every possibility being unactualized. There are incompatibilities of nonrealization as well as of realization; some possibility must be actualized, and this, in terms of our definition of deity, means that God must exist in some actual state or other.

Is the foregoing a proof of the reality of God? No, it is a disproof of both empirical atheism and empirical theism, of the age-old attempt to treat the theistic question as one of fact. There remains, not yet refuted, a priori theism and positivism (the view that 'deity' as defined lacks consistent significance, other than emotional or pictorial). To combat this last one must argue, not from facts but from concepts (other than that of God). We must say that it is no mere fact which the atheist or positivist is by implication denying, but our basic conceptions, those we use even in talking about fairyland. The antitheist, we may urge, is denying even the possibility of a fact.

In rejecting empirical arguments am I rejecting the Biblical pronouncement, "the heavens declare the glory of God"? No, not exactly that either. The heavens do declare the divine glory, but *for the believer*. Also, if the latter understands his belief, he sees that any conceivable heavens would declare it also. The actual heavens show only the particular form the divine creation has taken, a different heaven would show a different form; but to suppose that some odd or vicious world might exist which God could not have made is confusion. It splits possibility into two, that portion which is included in divine potentiality and that which is not. This is to limit the divine scope, exactly the aspect of the Unsurpassable (except by

self) which in consistency is subject to no limitation. Since any conceivable world, or possible
nonworld, by the definition of God, must be
possible content of divine experience, no argument should take the form, 'Because this possibility has been actualized, God exists, or
because that possibility has been actualized, God
does not exist'. All such talk is about a fetish,
not about God.

What the unbeliever who does not find the
divine glory in things must rather do is to
persuade himself that the definition of God is
logically (not factually) suspect—confused,
contradictory, or hopelessly vague. And he can
find plausible grounds for these charges. It is
precisely the coherence and clarity of the idea
of deity which 'proofs' must try to display.
Grubbing among facts is neither here nor there.
Self-understanding is the issue: someone is confused, either the theist, or the nontheist. Which
is it? This is the real question.

Note that we have here something like the
old doctrine: only faith can relate us to God.
Only the sense, trust, or insight that we really
mean something by our worship, and are not
talking nonsense, or chasing a formless pseudo-
conception can give the theistic answer. Observed facts and even laws of nature are neutral
to the topic. Laws are, by the definition of
'God', something like divine—that is, unsurpassably influential—decrees, free creations

which the universe is inevitably inspired to adopt. Given such and such laws, the theist conceives God making the corresponding decrees; given other laws, he simply conceives God making another set of decrees. Either way he thinks of God only as existent.

But suppose there were no laws? Who knows what this supposition means? Certainly we should not be there if it were true. Would anything thinkable, even 'there' be there? Here too, we have an issue of meaning. Could there be a simply lawless reality? Or simply no reality? Such questions are pseudo-factual, or in a broad sense logical, and so is the theistic question. 'Nothing' could not be 'there' (where?) and neither could the nonexistence of God. But perhaps God could be there (i.e., everywhere). And if he 'could' be, then he is. For no possibility can be put back of divine creativity, which *is* possibility. Or else nonsense.

But, you may say, perhaps it is nonsense? Just this the theistic 'proofs' must seek to discredit. It is their only task, except the related one of clarifying and explicating the non-nonsensical and coherent content of the Worshipful or Unsurpassable as such.

CHAPTER FOUR

Theism, Science, and Religion

For the believer, "the heavens declare the glory of God." The believing scientist can indeed think of himself as doing something like guessing the thoughts of God from the facts of nature. However, he must not take this to mean that God exists because of these particular facts, or because of God's having these particular thoughts, for this is blasphemous nonsense. But he may take it to mean that, for our contingent cosmic situation and us creatures in it, God has adopted certain contingent 'decrees' or intentions, concerning which we are neither totally in the dark nor securely and definitely 'in the know', but something in between, more or less sufficient for our needs.

The scientist seeing God in nature is more
than just a scientist, he is a philosopher or a religious man as well. He has a belief, not about
contingent nature and the actual state of science, but about any possible nature and any
possible science, that it must declare the glory
of God. Thus the issue between him and nonreligious scientists is deeper or more general
than any scientific issue. This is compatible
with his finding inspiration for his work in his
belief. Ultimately science, like human life itself,
derives from inspiration, as does effective ethical practice. Religion, it has been said, is "the
morale in morality." Unbelievers can of course
adopt ethical principles, but it may be hard for
them to keep up their courage, avoid idolatrous
substitutes for God, and yet master various
unethical emotions.

Similarly, a nontheist can do scientific work
of a high order, but he may lack the serene inspiration of a Kepler, saying that if God waited
millennia to be understood by him, Kepler, then
he, Kepler, could endure being misunderstood
for a while. Or of an Einstein speaking about
the "incarnate reason" in nature. Since man
lives on various levels of consciousness, there is
no clear-cut necessity that a creative scientist
must be religious in explicit belief. But that
there is an important connection seems broadly
supported both by a priori considerations and
by the history of discovery.

If I am correct in denying that the divine existence is an empirical matter, subject to conceivable empirical disproof, it must not be possible for any result of science, if it is really that, to conflict with theism. Obviously, evolutionary theory in biology does not do so; for to hold this is to assume that it would be incompatible with the unsurpassability of God that he should produce creatures in the gradual and partly-chance manner which neo-Darwinism infers from the observational facts. Where is the incompatibility? According to neoclassical theism, all creatures, and not just the creator, must be in some degree creative or partly free; hence in the cosmic interplay of innumerable acts of freedom there are bound to be aspects of disorder and partial randomness or chance. Einstein said, against indeterminism, that he could not believe "in a dice-throwing God." But to have free creatures is, in effect, to throw dice. So why not a dice-throwing God? I fear the great Albert—and great he was indeed—fell into the idolatry of identifying deity with absolute law or non-chance. We may be afraid of chance, but God need not be afraid even of that.

There seems nothing in quantum mechanics that conflicts with theism. If even particles have no wholly predetermined path, and atoms can change their internal organization, subject only to a statistical law, then creativity may indeed be universal. When classical physics appeared to deny this, it was functioning not as science but as philosophy, as a metaphysics. Absolute order, exhibited as such by nonabsolute observations, is a confusion. Newtonian physics, taken literally and absolutely, was an antitheistic metaphysics, resting not on observation but on illicit absolutizing of the observationally known. Only so could it have antitheistic implications.

Relativity physics is a puzzling case for my thesis, the most puzzling indeed of all. If reality is ultimately a self-surpassing process, embraced in a self-surpassing divine life, there must be something like a divine past and future. According to relativity physics, there is indeed, for our localized experience, a definite cosmic past and a definite cosmic future, but not a definite cosmic present. We may have two contemporaries out in space, one of which is years in the past of the other. And there seems no way to divide the cosmic process as a whole into past and future. Yet if neoclassical theism is right, it seems there must, for God at least, be a way. What is God's 'frame of reference', if there is no objectively right frame of reference for the cut between past and future? I can only suppose that we have in this apparent conflict a subtler form of the illicit extrapolation to the absolute from observational facts. Somehow relativity as an observational truth must be compatible with divine unsurpassability.

I personally have difficulty in understanding how absolute nonrelativity, for example instantaneous transmission of a signal, or motion with infinite velocity, even makes sense, so that here too I suspect the issue would be with positivism, not atheism. Unless some sort of physical relativity is compatible with deity, theism cannot even be logically possible—such would be my guess as to the logic of this matter. In that case, the observational facts are wholly neutral, as I hold they really must be.

As Professor John B. Cobb has remarked to me, whereas the relativity of simultaneity is connected with the question of relative motions of systems within which observations are being made compared to events being observed, unit events themselves (Whitehead's 'actual entities') do not move but merely happen or become. This remark serves to remind us of the element of artificiality involved in science as such. The cosmos is observable only from a localized and movable station within itself—unless the observer be himself cosmic. But a cosmic observer is not a topic within physics, since the physicist cannot ask such an observer to report his findings. So long as no such report can be received, any suprarelative simultaneity which the cosmic observer might discern would not violate any law of physics, for it would not constitute infinite velocity in the physicists' sense. It scarcely seems reasonable to expect

localized observations alone to tell the whole
story about what a nonlocalized observer would
observe. And it is not logically possible that
any mere facts could conflict with the existence
of an unsurpassably cosmic individual, since
the mere possibility of such a conflict with fact
implies surpassability. Thus, once more, the
question is nonempirical in principle.

The cosmic observer would not move, since
it would always be everywhere (somewhat as
a man's consciousness is everywhere in some
limited area in his nervous system, rather than
localized in a point). Each of its observations
would be made in a single present, not a succes-
sion of presents, and would exhibit the cosmos
impartially, rather than in a perspective which
suppressed detail more and more as the things
observed were distant from some small region,
and which revealed a past more and more remote in time as the things were distant in space.
Is this impartiality possible? It is if Unsurpassable consciousness is possible. Whether it is
possible or no is not an empirical matter, but
one of insight or faith.

An analogy sometimes occurs to me. A piano
player moves, and is aware of moving, two
hands at once. What the right hand does is not
determined by what the left hand does, but by
the musical design which is back of both in a
kind of preestablished harmony. (Not of course
in the Leibnizian sense, for we are allowing

a pervasive aspect of indetermination or creaturely freedom, but in the neoclassical sense of
statistical causal principles, probabilities only,
so far as individual actions are concerned.) The
design makes it unnecessary for there to be
immediate influence of one hand's actions upon
the other's. Both are subject to the *same* influence, either the design as already fixed, or the
unitary feeling of the player. Given creaturely
freedom, absolute control of events is out of
the question anyway; hence the lack of interdependence between contemporaries which our
cosmos seems to exhibit is logically compatible
with such control as unsurpassable cosmic governance implies. Some cosmic design setting
limits to freedom is alone implied a priori, and
without such a design cosmic knowledge by
localized observers is unthinkable. Hence any
knowable cosmos would satisfy the theistic re-
quirement. And a simply unknowable cosmos—
unknowable to localized, and also to unlocal-
ized observation—has no relevance, so far as I
can see, to any real problem.

There is a conceivable teleological justification for relativity. What good would it do us to
be able to transmit messages with infinite
velocity? It is bad enough being able to learn
about troubles around the world in seconds, but
to get bad news quickly from remote planets, and
have to reply almost at once—that would be too
much. Thank God we are isolated by the cos-

mically slow speed of light—we have enough complexity on our hands with this planet. Thus, once more, the heavens declare the glory of God; but so, in some appropriate way, would any possible heavens.

Both in Greece and in India, the analogy was sometimes used between an animal organism and deity. But rarely if ever was there adequate clarity about the two-way influence between a mind or 'soul' and its body. That soul 'rules' or should rule the body was clear to Plato, Aristotle, and the Hindu Ramanuja. But the rather obvious fact that the members of the body (microscopic in their real units) act upon the soul was strangely neglected or even denied outright.

A similar blindness concerning the political analogy was also remarkably pervasive. A 'ruler' is the eminent influence in his society, but not in any sense the sole influence. And the better the ruler, the more sensitively he responds to significant influences coming to him from the ruled. Ruling is interaction, not mere action. We act in one-way fashion upon posterity; and for that very reason we do not rule posterity. (So simple are some of the relevant analogies neglected by our forefathers!)

Assuming an interaction between human mind and human brain or nerve cells or molecules, and admitting God's interaction with every creature, we can say that each creature is to God somewhat as a nerve cell is to us. But of course the cosmos as organism, or as nervous system, is a radically unique case. For it alone has no external environment, or it alone is, as it were, a nervous system not encased in any further body. Moreover, it alone is unborn and undying.

It appears from the foregoing that a theist must not take the view of some scientific materialists that what a man does is simply what his atoms do, that causation is entirely on the micro-level. For then the interaction of God with his creatures could have no analogy to that of a man with his bodily constituents, and indeed 'the man interacts with other individuals' would be merely shorthand for, 'atoms interact'. But if a theist holds to an interactionist view of organisms, then he can apply the same transcendental categories to God and the creatures we know best, ourselves.

There is a certain attraction for scientists in the materialistic view above specified. I recently noticed the phrase, 'so uneconomical a theory as [mind-body] interactionism' in an essay by a scientist, or philosopher of science. But the consideration that a system of atoms whose collective behavior is wholly explicable in terms of the interactions of these atoms is simpler than one in which a full explanation must also take into account certain human experiences associated with the atomic events is no evidence that

nature consists only of the simpler type of
system. It establishes not even the slightest
probability of such a conclusion. Our intellectual convenience is one thing, the constitution
of nature is another. And the experiences are
given facts. Naturally it is simpler for a physicist to suppose that they play no causal role.
But what of that? The methodological rule,
'seek simplicity', is vicious unless it is followed
by the Whiteheadian injunction 'and mistrust
it'. Nature is very complex indeed, and we
are forever tempted to underestimate this
complexity.

A scientific friend of mine argues that the
unity of the cosmic organism is of a loose kind
since, while interactions can go through a brain
in a fraction of a second (and this explains the
time length of the human 'specious present'),
the cosmic interactions take billions of light
years, and so a cosmic consciousness, my friend
argues, must detect as little of what happens
in any shorter time as we do of what happens
in less than a tenth or twentieth of a second.
However, this is to overlook the differences in
principle to which the analogy, when applied
to the supreme case, is subject. As Plato pointed
out, an animal adjusting to an external environment is one thing, an 'ideal animal' adjusting
only to its own members, quite another. All the
clearer is this difference if we recall that the
inclusive organism is temporally as well as

spatially universal, i.e., ungenerated and immortal. There is a difference in principle between ephemeral and primordial-everlasting individuality. A man in dreamless sleep is not furnishing his body its unity of action, he is not forming its habits by decisions of his own, and thus at such times is not in any degree its 'lawgiver'. And at all times there are fundamental laws which obtain in his body thanks to no decisions of his. Thus the man's individuality as a sentient and conscious being is rather superficially imposed upon his bodily members. But the concrete individuality of the cosmos in its present distinctive laws (compared to other conceivable cosmic laws) is far from a superficial aspect of what goes on in a human body, or anywhere else. The cosmic laws either have no explanation at all, and are sheer brute facts, or they are explicable as the decisions of a cosmic mind, which never sleeps, and which gives rise to the basic habits of nature.

True, the cosmic consciousness must be sensitive to, or in detail dependent upon, the processes of nature. But only for inessential details, not for its essential identity or existence, this being noncontingent, or without alternative. Thus the dependence of God upon the world is superficial, while that of the world upon God is profound; by contrast, the dependence of an ordinary animal upon its bodily members is profound. Accordingly, the cosmic interaction in its particular character, for instance any particular speed, cannot be required for the very existence of God defined as unsurpassable by another.

What then is the significance of the slow tempo of cosmic interaction? If, as I hold, the business of a supreme creative power is to set the stage for lesser types of creativity which the supreme creativity can take into its own endlessly enriched life, there are two questions about the tempo of cosmic interaction: does it make possible coherent forms of creaturely experience, and will these furnish a coherent spectacle for the supreme spectator to enjoy? I see no reason why our cosmos cannot fulfill both requirements. Indeed any coherent cosmos, i.e., any cosmos, would do so.

On the one hand, surely the laws of nature set the stage for orderly nondivine experiences, which are unhampered by the time it takes for a signal to traverse the universe. There is no need for us, for instance, to be able to influence and be influenced quickly by inhabitants of remote planets. So I think the cosmic system is as unified as we need it to be. Moreover, looking at it from the other end—the cosmic body as making possible the cosmic consciousness—all that is required is that the cosmic panorama be capable of being experienced as a single picture, so to speak. And even we can (in abstract outline) almost do that. So why not the divine mind? I see the laws of nature, any laws of nature, as exactly what is required to make all that happens a possible object of one experience. They guarantee the individual unity of the cosmos as one. They do not guarantee my individual unity—which is a special thing within the cosmos, a derivative and expendable thing, while the cosmic unity or individuality is in principle primordial and indispensable. The only 'acts of God' we can identify (in spite of the lawyers) are the laws of nature. They make possible collectively coherent creative actions by the nondivine individuals and just this is the intent and need of the divine individual.

By various routes we arrive at the conclusion: any possible universe or state of affairs, any which can be coherently conceived as possible at all, would be a possible object of divine experience, so that the existence of God is not an empirical question at all, and not a scientific one. Scientific questions concern God only in terms of the kind of world, and corresponding kind of world-experiences, which he may be supposed to have. Not, 'Does he exist with some world or other', but only, 'With what world?' is the empirical or observational question. The rest is logic, in a broad sense, not fact.

The relations of theism to religion seem, if possible, more puzzling than its relations to science. Religion is much more than worship in the idealized sense so far discussed. It is the particular, social-historical-institutional form of worship found on this planet, and in various countries and cultures. Here immensely important empirical factors enter, entirely additional to worship merely as such, and to God merely as such, factors concerning which a mere metaphysician may be no wiser, or less wise, than anyone else. I find something which I seem to sense as revelation in the Bible, but then I also seem to find it in the still earlier hymns of Ikhnaton, and some Hindu and other non-Christian writings. However, in some respects at least other traditions seem less than equal to the Judeo-Christian in the clarity with which they depict the content of worship. For one thing, compared to Hinduism and Buddhism, Judaism, Christianity, and Islam seem freer from the substitution of self-deification for the worship of God. Here the Old Testament, I confess, seems to me a safer guide even than the New. Job addressed from the whirlwind is clear that he is not the deity; and so, I think, should we be. But with the Hindu and the Buddhist one must sometimes wonder.

Of course these things are subtle and disputes about them are always at least partly semantic. The unborn and undying deity is *in* each of us, and if by 'the true self' the Buddhist or Hindu (they often seem indistinguishable at this point) means this birthless and deathless element, then each of us houses the eternal one. 'That art thou'—yes, each of us is at least that. But He is also more! For mere timeless being is but an abstraction; the supreme reality is supreme creative becoming, forever enriching itself. An ordinary creature is but a fragment of the Creature, the divine process enriched by the de facto universe. Even such a fragment is more than the bare eternal, pure 'Being'; but it is incomparably less than the inclusive Creature, the living contemporary deity.

If by 'the true self' one means, that which the individual, when he understands himself, wishes to serve with all his being, then indeed this is the one universal God. Yet even here things are not so simple as mystics sometimes suggest. For the concrete deity which I can serve here and now is not unqualifiedly identical with the concrete deity which you can serve where you are. The genetic identity of the divine personality is not a simple unity, but an integration of a very real multiplicity of states and of lives sympathetically participated in.

In the Old Testament the Covenant is with Israel, a society, not a heap of individuals. Paul's metaphor of the social organism, whose parts are members one of another, continues this tradition. The chief novelty of the New Testament is that divine love, which seems plainly affirmed in the prophetic doctrine of a merciful deity concerned with the fate of the helpless and unfortunate, is carried to the point of participation in creaturely suffering, symbolized by the Cross taken together with the doctrine of the Incarnation. I personally see such participation as logically required by any intelligible doctrine of omniscience, since concrete awareness of another's suffering can, so far as I understand these things, only consist in participation in that suffering. But this implication of the idea of an all-comprehending Life needs to be made fully explicit, and Christian symbolism seems precious at this point.

Some theologians argue that the New Testament message is not just that God suffers *with* us, but that he suffers *for* us, as it were grieves over our mistakes and misfortunes. But this too seems to me implicit in the monotheistic doctrine, from Ikhnaton down. If anyone is clearly aware of the loss to the creatures through creaturely actions, it must be the divine spectator. And the only way to be aware of a loss as such is to regret it.

It seems implicit if not explicit in Christianity generally, and in Islamic doctrine also, though less clearly, that the social structure of existence is no mere appearance of something more ultimate, but an aspect of reality itself or as such. The Trinity is one attempt, perhaps none too successful, to express this. If interaction inheres in individuality as such, and if the concrete states of individuals are in principle dependent upon past states of individuals (not alone those

in the past of the same individual), and if what
is neither individual nor concrete state is a mere
abstraction, then the entire notion of a relation-
less absolute, devoid of inner plurality, the 'One'
of Plotinus, the 'Absolute' of Bradley, the 'Self'
of some forms of Hinduism, is an idolatrous
abstraction, when taken as self-sufficient or as
the most admirable object of contemplation.
Love is not derivative or secondary, but is itself,
in the highest form, the highest beauty. Here
the Greeks and the Orient tended to err, but
Ikhnaton the Egyptian was already clear. The
idea that love seeks what is more than love,
say the formless Nothing or Void or Absolute
Beauty, is a philosophical superstition. Love
seeks only further objects to love, and these
objects themselves embody love. The beauty of
the cosmos is the spectacle of its innumerable
forms of creative social experience, all basically
in harmony together; and this spectacle only
Eminent love can adequately inspire or enjoy.
What Eminent love 'desires' is only its own further participation in creaturely experiences,
themselves all forms of social experience, more
or less harmonious, all poised somewhere between pure love and pure hate or indifference
(which could not be distinguished).

A dubious side of the New Testament, as it
has actually affected religious life, is the im-
mense stimulus it gave, partly through Paul's
speculations, to the idea that our chief concern

should be over what happens to us after death.
Here, as at some other points (not all!), the
influence of Plato was not exactly helpful. The
conception of an immortal soul, imprisoned in
the body, and with its earthly career but an
incident in its ultimate destiny, is Platonism not
at its best; it exhibits the partly life-hating and
life-fearing Plato, or the legislator Plato, who
is tempted to think of providence as an exten-
sion of our earthly legal codes. The wicked
must—he perhaps thought—face a reckoning
more adequate than they usually find in this
life, and the good must have something better
to expect than any rewards that fickle fortune
and fickle human opinion are likely to bestow
upon them. But all arguments for personal
immortality, as most philosophers and theologians have conceived this, seem to me fallacious; and I include ethical and religious
arguments. Even the argument from the words
of Jesus, "God is the God of the living not of
the dead," seems to turn upon a possible ambiguity. 'Abraham, Isaac, and Jacob' are indeed
in one sense 'living not dead', for immortalized
in God are not their mere corpses, but their
lives between birth and death. Of course, too,
'soul', life or mind, *as such* is immortal, for it
is the principle of all reality and unreality, all
motion and all permanence. Also one Eminent
Life or Mind is deathless and unborn.

Perhaps I have a blind spot in this region, but I see no need for post-terrestrial rewards or punishments—beyond the satisfaction, to be achieved now, of feeling one's earthly actuality indestructibly, definitively, appropriated in the divine participation. If, or insofar as, punishments or rewards are necessary to secure good behavior, our human laws, magistrates, and institutions should if possible be shaped to provide them in this life. But that God has to guide and inspire the world by these none too efficient means I cannot believe. God deals directly with each creature 'in his heart'. The divine 'laws' need no backing by 'sanctions'. The reward of virtue, so far as it can in the ethical sense be rewarded, is truly 'virtue itself'. He who does not love God and his neighbor for God's and his neighbor's sakes does not love them—period. And if he does not, what reward does he, in the religious sense, 'deserve'? So those who need the reward will not deserve it! And is the way to persuade us into love for God or anyone to frighten us with possible penalties? Also, if the penalty works, do we love God and our neighbor, or only our escape from the penalty? The reward for loving God is simply that he alone is unqualifiedly lovable. This is the whole of the matter. It is now, each moment, that we miss the pearl of great price by not loving him.

Connected with this point, however, I incline
to look to the Buddhists in one way, and to the
Jews of the Old Testament, in another way, as
counterbalance to such horrible examples as
Dante—and I could almost add, St. Paul. I agree
with Buddhism that, strictly speaking, a person
is numerically a new entity each moment, so that
the person who wants to wake up in heaven to
begin a further life is not asking for his present
actuality to be preserved from death. That actuality is already largely gone the next moment—
unless God is preserving its full flavor forever.
But then perhaps no further immortality is
needed? The Jew who served God without asking for post-mortem rewards, or worrying about
post-mortem punishments, was to my mind
eminently sound.

One personality indeed must evermore go on
to new achievements, for only in this way can
any achievements endure. But this one immortality suffices; to demand more may be to play
at being God, or to try to make bargains with
deity.

Moreover, self-interest, concern for the personal future, is from the Buddhist-Whiteheadian
point of view only a special strand, a narrow
kind, of altruism—the interest which the present
self takes in those possible or probable future
selves which will bear the same name and pro-
long the same personal history. Any future-re-
garding interest is a sort of sympathy felt by

a momentary actuality for various potential future actualities. There is therefore no metaphysical and, I incline to think, no religious reason to make an undue fuss about the one strand of sympathy which relates present experience to future experiences of the same organism or the same personal history, and this no matter whether the future experiences are to be on earth or anywhere else. The present actuality enjoys its glimpse of the universe and the divine glory; what comes after transcends that actuality in any case, and interest in it may as well in principle transcend self-regard altogether. The future that ultimately matters is not particularly mine or yours, or even human, but cosmic and divine.

Perhaps our culture will find its way back after a long detour to the original Jewish insight that only two things matter, creaturely life between birth and death, and the unborn and undying life of God. The sole bargain or covenant to make with God is that we do our best and trust him to salvage what can be salvaged from our failures and to make the most that can be made of our successes. But he will do this for the cosmos and his own life, and for us only as items in the inclusive reality, members of the inclusive society. Does this mean that there is no divine love for us as individuals? Not at all, but it is love for us as we are, between birth and death, not for us as some magically different yet oddly identical entities after death. This, I think, is how we love ourselves and our friends most genuinely—as earthly realities between birth and death. The rest is vague, confused fantasy, not definite serious concern. God need not be so confused in his love for us as we in our fancied unearthly love for ourselves and our friends.

We may need to combine the Hindu-Buddhist insight into the relativity and tenuousness of human self-identity with the Old Testament insight that the sole indispensable self-identity is divine, taken as related to, rather than identical with, ours. We are ephemeral, but immortally so, for nothing escapes being woven into the imperishable and living texture of deity.

It is a mistranslation of this sublime doctrine to speak of our being 'absorbed' into God, or to call this form of immortality 'impersonal'. 'Absorbed' suggests a total loss of particular form; but no such loss is in question, since it is particulars in their particularity which are preserved in God. Also what is personal if not an actual human life from birth to death? It is this which is everlastingly cherished.

To say (as I have known some to do) that it is 'no help to us' that God enjoys us forevermore is to say either that we have no need to know that we achieve any really permanent results by our efforts, or else that a good to God is of no concern to us. In other words, it is to say either that the demand of reason for an aim which retains its attractiveness when the whole truth, including truth about the future, is taken into account does not concern us, or else that we love God not one whit. Yet by definition God is wholly, unsurpassably lovable. In short, such contentions are wild talk, without regard to the meaning of the question under discussion.

Finitude, limited scope, birth and death, constitute the definiteness or concreteness of our lives, as contrasted with God's. He who rebels against death wishes to be God. But only God can be God, infinitely able to adapt to changing circumstances. Our privilege is to love and serve him, not to *be* him. Yet we may trust him to see to it that death, like 'finis' at the end of a book, no more means the destruction of our earthly reality than the last chapter of a book means the destruction of the book. We write our book of life either for extremely inadequate and ultimately, according to all rational probability, nonexistent readers, or for the one adequate Reader. Some have little chance to write much of a book, some make less than the best use of the chance they have. But chance, multiple freedom, existence, God, are mutually implicative ideas.

Freud was right in saying, "the world is not a Kindergarten." But it could not be. Or if it could be and were, the opportunities in such a world must be as trivial as the risks. So we should accept our risk-full world as essentially good and providential. It is for us to minimize, by our own wisdom, energy, courage, and good will, the most destructive risks, not for us to call upon God to upset death by miracle so that the neglected children of men may have a second and better chance. Einstein's rejection of a 'dice-throwing God' was a great man's error. And human individuals are some of the dice; for being, in Plato's language, 'souls', they are 'motions that move themselves'. In short, they are lesser creators, sparks of the unsurpassable creativity, which is infinitely more than the mere 'ground of being', for it is also the inclusive fruition of being, the sublime and universal Creature.

The question of the legendary bright child, 'Who made God'? has an answer. God in his concrete de facto state is in one sense simply self-made, like every creature spontaneously springing into being as something more than any causal antecedents could definitely imply. In another sense, or causally speaking, God, in his latest concrete state, is jointly 'made' or produced by God and the world in the prior states of each. We are not simply co-creators, with God, of the world, but in last analysis co-creators, with him, of himself. As the Socinians, Fechner, Lequier, Varisco, Berdyaev, and a few others saw, while the proud scholarly world in general as yet could not see, to do anything at all is to do something to God, to decide anything is to decide something divine. For it is to determine something of the content of the all-inclusive awareness. Our deeds are instantly written in strictly indelible ink. And we have a part in the writing. As the humble, earnest poet had it,

> All are architects of fate . . .
>
> For the structure that we raise
> Time is with materials filled.
> Our todays and yesterdays
> Are the blocks with which we build.

But presumably Longfellow believed also in a superarchitect without which our creativity could only produce mere confusion, that is, nothing, and apart from whom any order that, *per impossibile,* might appear momentarily could in the end leave not even an appreciable trace upon the face of things.

By recognizing ordinary, surpassable forms of creativity in their multiplicity we explain why disorder and conflict exist. By recognizing extraordinary, Unsurpassable Creativity and its strictly universal influence, we explain, as Plato long ago divined, how the disorders and frustrations can be within a basic order, and contribute to an overall transcendent Good, which in the *Timaeus* turns out to be no merely eternal pattern or form, but the concrete life of the Besouled

Animal, the soul which, as we are explicitly told, contains the cosmic body, not vice versa.

The only twentieth-century philosopher who recalls Plato to any striking degree, Whitehead, returns to this vision, but frees it from the corruptions which 'Platonism' subjected it to, and makes far clearer in what the 'self-motion' or creativity of mind or soul consists, and far clearer that and how *all* motion of singular individuals, mere aggregates apart, is of this kind. The problem of 'matter' and 'space' (or the 'receptacle') which Plato honestly admits deeply puzzles him, and which Aristotle seems to have thought he had intellectually mastered so far as this could be done, but which only a long painful process of collective inquiry could really illuminate, has at last proved not hopelessly recalcitrant to a genuinely platonic solution. Souls are indeed 'self-moved' (which in Greek really meant, self-changed, i.e., creative), and when (with Leibniz) we distinguish clearly between singulars or true individuals and aggregates, we can, as Plato apparently wished to do, see all motion as soul motion. We can also (with Fechner, Lequier, Varisco, Peirce, Bergson, Whitehead) see all causality as involving a kind of transcendence of merely mechanical order—some injection, however slight, of strictly unforeseeable novelty of concrete form, which will subsequently influence all future changes.

Taking one more step, and overcoming Leibniz's blunder of supposing monads to have 'no windows', no direct awareness of one another, we can explain influence among individuals as simply their awareness of one another by more or less unconscious 'prehensions'. Thus we have Plato's vision in the *Timaeus* and *Laws,* Book Ten, worked out for us in our intellectual climate. The rest is details.

Even the 'first monotheist' said much of what needs to be said. Addressing his all-loving deity as "fashioning thyself" Ikhnaton declares

> Thou of thyself art length of life;
> Men live through thee.

We have only to add the Platonic insight that we are not outside the cosmic life but in it to see that we too help to fashion deity. Creativity, prehending other creativity, endlessly deriving thus new materials for further emergent synthesis, and operating on both surpassable and (by others) unsurpassable levels accounts for good and evil, change and permanence, and gives a lasting meaning to all decision.

I should like to sum up the religious meaning of neoclassical theism by considering the oldest known discussion of the 'problem of evil', the Book of Job. 'Does Job serve God for naught'? was the initial question in that sublime book. It is too often overlooked that the implied answer was affirmative. The voice from the whirlwind promises Job nothing and threatens him with nothing. It merely calls his attention, somewhat humorously, to the grandeur and mystery of a cosmos in which man is but an item. Job seems finally to understand, not that his demands have an answer too deep for his comprehension, but that individual demands are not in order. We serve God, or we settle for a less rational aim, and if we do the former it should be because we want to have the right or reason-satisfying aim now, not because some less rational aim, like eventual personal advantage, will thereby be accomplished. There is no appropriate reward for serving God; simply there is nothing else (able to withstand criticism) for a conscious being to live for.

The voice from the whirlwind does not explicitly say that Job or his comforters were in error concerning divine justice. The voice says nothing about justice. It deals rather with the mystery of cosmic power. Job's mistake was in supposing that he knew what is meant by unsurpassable or divine power. No man has ever created a star, an element of nature, or an animal; nor has he ever governed a cosmos. How then, in the mouth of such a being, could words like 'create' or 'govern', applied to the cosmic situation, have any clear sense?

The shallow view of the divine rebuke to Job is that he is brought to admit that the relation between God's power and his goodness, or perhaps the goodness itself, is beyond human grasp. This interpretation supposes that at least we know what divine power is, and only its use by divine justice is too deep for us. However, is not this idea of divine power already, just in itself, quite as mysterious as that of divine justice? The mystery is in both terms and not simply in one, or simply in the relation between the one and the other. If we really knew what it would be like to create or rule cosmically, we should also know what it would be like to do so wisely or righteously, and vice versa. But can we know either?

A careless objection to the message from the whirlwind is that Job is overawed by a mere show of force, that he grovels before brute power. But the sublime thing about this ancient document is that there is not a hint or suggestion that the power is to be taken as a threat. Job is not warned to take care lest the power be used against him; and he is not invited to consider how it might be used to reward him should he submit and confess his mistake. The almost unbelievable nobility of this old writer shows in the dignity with which Job's disinterestedness is respected. He is not scared or bribed into humility, he is simply shown his actual cognitive situation. And what is that situation? That he has been brought up on a theory of all-mightiness whose meaning no one

understands. What is the use of trying to derive
consequences from a concept that one does
not possess? There was no clearly understood
notion of God's power to give rise to a problem
of evil, of why God 'does' this or 'does' that.
What does it mean to say, 'God does something'? To accept such language as clear, but
find a puzzle in the divine motive, *why* God
does things, is, as Berdyaev said, once for
all, to treat as a mystery a problem which one
has 'already overrationalized'. The puzzle
begins one step earlier. Human 'power' we
know something about, but what sort of
analogy enables us to speak of 'divine power'?
Until we have this analogy straight, there is no
clearly defined problem of evil.

Traditional theism and traditional atheism are
alike in this, that they overestimated the claims
of 'omnipotence' to constitute a well-defined
premise from which conclusions are deducible.
God's power or influence must of course be
worshipful, unsurpassably great; but to identify
this unsurpassability of power with its sheer
monopoly, a control by which all concrete details
of existence are determined, leaving the creatures with nothing to determine for themselves,
no genuine options of their own, is to burden
the divine worshipfulness with a logical paradox
of our own making. The monopoly theory is at
best no more than a theory. To worship God
need not be to accept the theory. But really, it is

less than a theory, for no one knows what it means.

To try to advance beyond the modesty of Job's final confession of incompetence may be rash, but perhaps not hopelessly so. Three millenia have passed. The entire ancient world produced no clear alternative to the monopoly notion of unsurpassable power. However, in our time there is an alternative. It is the view that supreme creativity implies lesser forms of creativity, and that the supreme form sets limits to the chance elements introduced by the lesser forms, but does not and could not eliminate all such elements. Perhaps there is no *why* God sends us evils, since he does not send them at all. Rather he establishes an order in which creatures can send each other particular goods and evils.

Apart from God nothing could make sense, even as evil. Only meaningless chaos, the same as nothing, fits the idea of a godless world. But on the other hand, God as sole form of creative freedom would be a meaningless perfection of order with nothing to order. Everything would be wholly under control, but this everything would be nonentity. That there is not perfect harmony and security is already explained by the notion of self-determining creatures, the only positively conceivable kind of creatures. What cannot be explained merely in this way, however, is that in spite of all discord and peril a

world of coexisting, and insofar mutually harmonious, things can exist and continue. This is
the providential aspect, that it all adds up to a
meaningful world.

Explanations of particular evils in terms of
individual deserts plus divine distributive ma-
chinery are, I believe, just wrong, a misuse of
the idea of providence. God is neither a wise
sadist nor a detached magistrate, torturing us
for some good end. Rather he turns creatures
loose to be each other's destiny, within wise
limits of natural law. Cosmic governance is not
a magnified law court. It is thrilling that one
ancient document cleanly rejects this theory.
Only Job's comforters, not the voice from beyond, espouse it. Job, enlightened, not terrified
or bribed, at least partially understands, perhaps, that there can be no moral why for
sufferings. Life could not be free of the risk of
unmerited sufferings. Alas, the level thus long
ago reached is still above multitudes of human
beings.

I cannot resist saying a word or two, in this
context, about Kafka's *The Castle*. Like Job,
Kafka finds the workings of providence abys-
mally mysterious. In the modern writer, however, the emphasis is upon the intermediaries
between any of us and the ultimate ruler of all
things. Concrete actions are taken only by
members of the bureaucracy interposed between the villagers and the unapproachable

aristocrat who owns the castle. And is it not true that our concrete destinies come to us from other creatures, more or less like ourselves? Job's sufferings came, not directly from God but from Satan, via the Sabaeans, the Chaldeans, lightning, wind, and also (as we might now say) bacteria and his own bodily cells. All of these were fellow creatures, not God. The universe is, in a manner of speaking, a bureaucracy, and the members of this bureaucracy whose actions furnish the setting for an individual's life are all fallible, more or less unintelligent, imperfect agents. After all, *they* are not divine. To suppose that divine infallibility and goodness can simply determine life's setting for each of us is to suppose that only one agent really acts, God himself. But in that case the word 'act' has no secular meaning, but only a mystical one, referring exclusively to deity. And then there is no rational problem of evil since, on the assumptions, secular reason can have no notion of divine power. If there is a secular conception of this power, then it is not a sheer monopoly and does not determine the concrete course of events. A host of intermediaries stand between any one of us and deity. Thus Kafka supplements Job in a helpful way, without himself, perhaps, necessarily seeing clearly how this is so. A monopoly of power is no ideal but, as I have said on other occasions, a nightmare, a ghastly semblance of meaning which, looked at soberly and analytically, exhibits its inherent absurdity. In any possible world one would depend, for the details of one's existence, upon fellow creatures and one's own past acts. From this solidarity of destiny, this partial dependence upon the choices of others, there is no escape, in this world or any other. Any kingdom of heaven must incorporate this aspect.

As Berdyaev, with his usual courage and penetration, insisted, not only must the creatures derive concrete details from other creatures, but God himself must be qualified by creaturely choices. To know what the creatures decide to do is to be Himself in his cognitive state decided by these decisions. God can know what we freely decide only because we do so decide. Thus our contingency becomes also his. Our freedom is in a measure, in Buber's words, 'divine destiny'. There is chance and tragedy even for God. This is part of what creaturely freedom means.

Yet the essential necessity of the divine essence and existence is not thereby infringed. God, the unsurpassable, exists no matter what anyone decides. His nonexistence is inconceivable, and he who is unable to conceive this inconceivability is unable to conceive God. But that in God to which there is no conceivable alternative is the merest abstraction, by itself. God is unimaginably more than the mere existence of that which could not fail to exist. He is the contingent actuality which fully expresses all actuality, in an unsurpassable adequacy of love for all. He who does not conceive this actuality, which might have been infinitely otherwise than it is, also does not conceive God.

As the merely contingent is a concrete 'fetish' or 'idol', so the merely necessary is an abstract one. That philosophers often explicitly espouse the latter sort of idolatry, while primitive or naive persons tend to fall into the former, is to be expected. What is more surprising is that many philosophers have unwittingly, or by implication, fallen also into the naive or concrete form of fetishism—by their rejection of anything like an ontological proof, or their search for an empirical proof or disproof for the bare existence of the unsurpassable individual. They have thereby assimilated the individual presupposition of all existence to the individuals subsequent to that presupposition; they have demoted the universal creator to the status of mere creature. Or, they have looked for the very principle of factuality as though it were itself just another fact.

If natural theology can simultaneously avoid both the abstract and the concrete forms of idolatry, and also avoid the absurd attempt to exalt the supreme creativity by treating ordinary creativity as nothing, it may be expected to have a new vitality and a new power to deal with its critics. Plato said that there had always been atheists. Perhaps there always will be some in civilized societies. But perhaps also we know at last how rationally to answer them.

CHAPTER FIVE

Epilogue: Abstract and Concrete Approaches to Deity and the Divine Historicity

It is hard to be certain, but apparently Dr. Bultmann holds that we cannot attribute anything like 'historicity' to God.[1] However, according to neoclassical (dipolar) theism or panentheism, only something extremely abstract can be purely eternal, and all concrete reality, even divine, is in a broad sense historical. As Berdyaev, Heidegger, Barth, and many others have said or hinted, there is something like a 'divine time'.

[1]This Epilogue is republished by permission from the *Union Seminary Quarterly Review* 20 (1965) pp. 265-270, where it appeared in conjunction with a discussion between Rudolf Bultmann and Schubert Ogden.

Of course God is unborn and immortal. This is part of his being 'unsurpassable by another', which is by far the best simple explication of 'God', in addition to 'the one worshipped'. Only beginningless and endless duration is unsurpassable duration. The unsurpassability itself, simply as such, is immutable; that is, God could not begin, or cease, to be unsurpassable. Nevertheless, neither the concrete life of deity nor any life whatever can be immutable. There are, however, various kinds of mutability. Ordinary individuals may change by increasing, or decreasing, or remaining about the same, in value; God can only increase. He cannot become inferior, even to himself, but he can and endlessly does surpass himself, as well as all others. He is strictly *all-surpassing*. This means that in some sense he has a past and a future. What must be denied is only past and future in the deficient forms found in human life (for instance). The past as much more largely forgotten than remembered, the future as poorly understood, or as cause of fretful anxiety, also the past as extending back of one's own birth, or the future as extending beyond one's own death—these and related deficiencies are not divine. (Berdyaev is helpful here.) But it is faulty analysis which identifies past and future as such with these deficiencies.

With Fausto Sozzini, Fechner, Pfleiderer, Lequier, Berdyaev, and others I reject as idolatry the identification of God with 'the absolute', 'infinite', 'immutable', or 'necessary'. God is on both sides of such abstract contraries, and only so can he be more than a mere abstraction. He is finite *and* infinite, eternal *and* temporal, necessary *and* contingent, each in suitable and unique respects. The Greeks tended to worship the eternal or necessary as such, but we need not do so.

How, Dr. Bultmann queries, do we derive the idea of God? In several ways. The recognition of ourselves as beings surpassable by others in power, wisdom, duration, and other positive traits yields, by simple contrast, that of the being *un*surpassable by others. 'God' is the name for the one who is unsurpassable by any conceivable being other than himself. Anselm almost but not quite discovered this. He partly failed to do so because he thought, with late Greek thought, that God must be unsurpassable absolutely. But on the contrary, the one whom all should worship needs only to be secure against rivalry by another. That he can surpass himself is quite compatible with his being worshipped by all, so long as it is *impossible* that he should fail to surpass all others as well.

In the foregoing, the idea of God is derived in two ways. First, from the understanding of 'surpassable by others' one derives, by mere negation, the idea of 'unsurpassable by others'.

True, one could, from the idea of 'surpassable by self', derive that of 'unsurpassable by self'; and then one could put the two forms of unsurpassability together to constitute the idea of absolute unsurpassability. And this is in effect what most metaphysicians have done. But in this they were begging an important philosophical question: Is the notion of an absolute maximum of reality and value, in every sense unsurpassable, any more consistent than the pseudo-ideas of 'greatest possible number' or 'greatest possible magnitude'? The antinomies which are deducible from the alleged notion of a 'most real being' (the classical sense of 'perfection') should by now have taught us that this is another pseudo-idea, a mere absurdity. Yet the idea of a being unsurpassable by another has not been shown to yield antinomies, and for all we know is not absurd.

The second mode of derivation of the idea of God is from the idea of worship as such. Anselm saw that worship implies the absolute exclusion of rivalry between the worshipper and the worshipped. (If we could conceive a superior to God we should either have to worship that superior, were it only a mere possibility, or else find ourselves unable to worship at all.) To see this as clearly as he saw it was a sign of genius. It was also a sign of genius (at best poorly understood by most modern philosophers) to see that this exclusion of rivalry implies not just the factual exclusion of nonexistence but the a priori exclusion of the bare logical possibility of nonexistence. Why this great discovery was so little understood I have tried to explain elsewhere (in *Anselm's Discovery*).

The harmony between the two derivations of 'unsurpassable by another' is a confirmation of both. There are also other ways of deriving the idea.

Are we objectifying or conceptualizing God in saying the foregoing? No more than we make a man a mere object or mere concept when we say that any man is surpassable by others as well as by himself. Those we love, other than God, are surpassable; God, whom we love, is unsurpassable, save by himself. But in neither case are those we love bare surpassability, or bare unsurpassability, as such, the mere abstractions. No individual whatever can be exhausted in a concept or definition. And no still living individual has a determinate quality fully defined once for all, since each moment of life is creative and produces a new concrete version of the individual's distinctive quality. This creative inexhaustibility applies supremely to God. And with him the qualification 'still living' is needless, since he can never fail to be living. So God is always, for that reason alone, more than any 'object' to be pointed to (*vorhanden*). But in addition, mere thought cannot give us even the past of an individual in its fullness. Thought is schematic, giving at most an outline of reality. Only perception or encounter gives us full concreteness, so far as we can possess it at all. And with human beings this is not very far, since conscious human perception is also in various ways schematic. Finally, since God is the inclusive concrete reality, he is least of all exhaustible by any concept or conscious human percept.

Concepts About God

But how does all this prevent us from having some abstract concepts *about* God, correct so far as they go? I see nothing in Kierkegaard or Buber to justify the negative view here. 'Unsurpassability by another' suffices to distinguish the divine reality, whatever it may be in its fullness, from the character of any nondivine individual. Insofar as we encounter God perceptually (and he, being *ubiquitous,* must be encountered somehow in all experience), we encounter, not mere unsurpassability, but something infinitely richer in determinations than this bare abstraction. Yet, since abstractions need not pretend to be more than just that, I fail to see why they must be rejected just because unspeakably more is also true of what the abstractions, so far as they go, describe.

Dr. Bultmann was once asked, in my hearing, 'What is the difference between the God of philosophy and the God of religion'? His reply, which pleased me greatly, was, if I recall correctly, approximately this: 'The God of philosophy is anyone's God, the God of religion is your God and mine'. I should generalize a bit more widely, and say, the God of philosophy, or at least of metaphysics, is any creature's God, the God of religion is the God of humanity, or more concretely, our God now. (Paul Weiss has expressed a somewhat similar distinction in his *The God We Seek*.) Each man must relate *himself* to God if he wants the full value of belief, and no concept can capture the concrete quality of this 'himself', much less of the God of himself. Since, on the neoclassical view, God is infinitely responsive to each creature, 'my God' is far from being identical with the God of creatures in general, or even with the God of Abraham. It is the same divine individual, but not the same individual in the same 'state'. (To reject such distinctions as inapplicable to God is merely one manifestation of the Greek error which I find in much traditional metaphysics.) Concerning 'our God' all talk is confessional, but not concerning the God of creatures in general. For *that* God is inherent in all basic secular conceptions, and only intellectual inhibitions can keep the idea from being formulated.

Human beings are individuals who interact with or influence one another. They thus form one another's *Mitwelt*. (I believe, and Buber seems to hint, that ultimately the *Umwelt* is entirely *Mitwelt*, a matter which need not be further considered here.) But human beings do this in surpassable ways only. Some do it for a longer time than others, or with more wisdom both in wielding and in responding to influences. And some have less power than others to maintain their own integrity through a wide variety of *Mitwelten* or *Umwelten*. That this power is, in all of us, limited or surpassable is the same as to say that we are born and die. And with all of us the scope of our giving and receiving influences is less than cosmic, which is the same as to say that we are localized beings, 'in space' but not ubiquitously so. To say all this is already virtually to have, by contrast, the idea of an individual interacting with others, not for a time but always, not with some but with ideal wisdom, not with a mixture of love, hate, and indifference, but with unsurpassable love for all. This is all included in saying that surpassable modes of interaction are intelligible only if unsurpassable ways are also intelligible. And this already defines deity. 'Eternity' is implied just so far as it is required to exclude rivalry by another. Analysis shows that self-surpassing and a supe-

rior kind of change are not only compatible
with, but required by, this exclusion.

Traditional metaphysics was too enamored
of the supposed idea of an absolute, immutable
maximum to follow out the inherent logic of
the idea of unsurpassable individual (or unsurpassable subject of interaction—they are
really the same). It was held that while ordinary individuals interact, God's superiority is
that he acts only, and does not interact. Unfor-
tunately, this destroys all analogy between God
and creatures, and it contradicts the very meaning of worship and related religious ideas. Nor
is there any justification for the notion that
interaction, as compared to simple action, indi-
cates a weakness. Man's sensitivity to influences
is just as superior to that of the lesser creatures
as is his power over them, and analysis shows
that the two superiorities belong logically together. Similarly, the gulf between us and God
is no less shown in the limitations of our responsiveness to, than in those of our power
over, others. But metaphysicians for two millennia almost unanimously missed all this and
dogmatized instead about the 'superiority of
agent to patient', or of cause to effect, immutable to mutable, self-sufficient or independent to dependent. This procedure was, I
believe, equally bad as philosophy and as
theology.

I do not know how far Dr. Bultmann is aware of the radical break between this new kind of metaphysics and the old. One thing is sure: if the new kind is wrong, it must be for partly new reasons. For the new, unlike the old, makes no leap from time to mere eternity, from the relative to the merely absolute, from interacting individuals to an impassible one, from the dependent to the wholly self-sufficient. The new issues, whatever they are, are less simple. Only a fresh inquiry can deal with them. I do not find this inquiry in Heidegger, whose career I have followed since I first heard him lecture at Freiburg in 1924.

How far all this is even intelligible to one brought up largely in the German tradition I can scarcely guess. But at least two German writers seem to be largely on my side, Fechner (in the great chapter on "God and the World" in his *Zendavesta)* and Pfleiderer (in his *Grundriss*). Heidegger's hint that not mere eternity but infinite temporality may be the key to the idea of God I take, with Ogden, to point toward panentheism.[2] But I think it is a mistake, for reasons given above, to restrict theology, as Heidegger seems to do, to confession, to deny natural theology altogether. It is only religion, concrete dealing with God by concrete

[2]*Sein und Zeit,* 8th edition, 1957, p. 427; English edition, London, 1962, p. 499.

groups or individuals, that is nontheoretical, and a sheer addition to any metaphysics. But abstract dealings with God, claiming to be no more than that, are another matter.

If I have called God an 'individual', this is with the understanding that, as the unique because unsurpassable individual, he is also absolutely cosmic or universal in his capacities, interacting with *all* others, relevant to *all* contexts, and in this sense absolutely universal —the only strictly universal individual, or individual universal. (This is by no means Hegel's 'concrete universal'; for God as concrete is unimaginably more than God in his bare individuality. The concrete is God as in some contingent actual state related to some actual state of the world.) 'Being' is God as enjoying creatures: the creatures he does enjoy are the actual beings, along with the enjoyment itself as the inclusive being; the creatures he might enjoy, along with the possible ways in which he might enjoy them, are the possible forms of being.

It is truly amazing how superior Anselm's definition, when clarified to allow for self-surpassing, proves itself to be as guide to metaphysical and theological problems, compared to the more usual definitions in terms of simple perfection or absoluteness. Amazing indeed, considering how nearly unanimously natural theologians have preferred these other definitions! And critics of natural theology have done much the same. They too have supposed that Deity must be the transcendental snob, or the transcendental tyrant, either ignoring the creatures or else reducing them to his mere puppets, rather than the unsurpassably interacting, loving, presiding genius and companion of all existence.

Index

absolute, x, 21, 24; God as, 54, 66, 69f., 106, 128;
   see also unsurpassability
abstract, God as, 27, 43ff., 60, 74, 77, 106
actuality, as finite, 21; divine, 72, 74, 124
adaptation, unlimited power of, 39
agent and patient, 134
agnostics, 6
all-inclusive, 16, 20, 28, 105
all-knowing, 45, 72, 85
all-powerful, 45
animal innocence, 6; instinct, 57
animals, lower, 4ff.
Anselm, St., x, 17, 18, 20, 50, 52, 128, 129, 136
antinomy, Kant's first, 28
a priori, xi, 4, 51f., 68, 77f.
Aquinas, St. Thomas, 2, 44, 50, 67
argument, cosmological, 50, 67; design, 49f., 53, 57ff., 67;
   from beauty, 53; global or religious, 49; moral, 48, 54;
   ontological, 39, 50ff., 124
arguments for God, a priori, 66; empirical, x, 67
Aristotle, 14, 28, 97, 115
atheism, empirical, 87
atoms, 57, 98

Barth, K., x, 126
beauty, absolute, 15, 106; and God, 106

becoming not inferior, 25; in God, 104
being, 25; God as, 136
Berdyaev, N., 113, 119, 123, 126, 127
Bergson, H., 115
Bible, 8, 9, 87, 103ff., 106
body, God's, 98ff.
Brightman, E. S., 67
Buber, M., 123, 131, 133
Buddhism, 22, 109
Bultmann, R., 126ff., 132, 135

Carneades, 58
category mistake, 62
causa sui, man as, 10
causality, 60, 115
cause, xi; God as, 60; uncaused, 44
caused, God as, 44, 60
chance, 57, 92, 112f.
change not a weakness, 18
chaos, limits to, 64
Christianity, 7, 103
class, necessarily nonempty, 64
classical theism, 68
Cobb, J. B., 94
co-creators, 113
completeness, 16-19
concrete, God as, 37, 51, 61, 113, 136f.
contingent qualities of God, 27, 44, 50, 90
create, 9ff., 26
creation, 70, 80
creationist philosophy, 58, 82
creativity, 26, 114f.
creator, 9, 16, 26, 84, 124; creature as, 26, 81f., 113ff.;
        man as, 10f.
creature, the inclusive, 104, 113

Dante, 109
death, triumph over, 56
decrees, God's, 90
Descartes, R., 50, 52
determinable, ultimate, 74
determinism, 26, 96

effect, God as, 60
Einstein, A., 91, 92, 113
eminent love, 106
empirical, 41, 52; defined, 67; God as, 52
empiricist, 83
eternal, God as, 3, 44, 103f., 133, 135
evil, problem of, 62, 80ff., 116-128; utterly senseless, 80
evolution, 92
existence of God, 85; as eternal, 52; as necessary,
    20, 25, 50, 59, 67, 86, 102; not same as actuality, 76
experience of God, 2, 31

faith, 31, 88
Fechner, G. T., 72, 113, 115, 127, 135
finite wholes, 7
finitistic, 28
fragmentariness, 6ff.
freedom, multiple, 59, 60, 74, 96, 102, 112, 123
Freud, S., 32, 112
future in God, 127

great exception, God as, 33, 37
greatest, actuality, 66; number, 20, 43; value, 20, 42, 129

Hegel, G. W. F., 37, 137
Heidegger, M., 126, 135
Hinduism, 23, 103, 106
Hocking, W. E., 7
humanists, 6
humanity as object of worship, 6
Hume, D., xi, 25, 27, 28, 35, 52, 85

idea of God, as rational, 37; how derived, 128
idol, 86; abstract, 124
idolatry, 11, 74, 79, 124
Ikhnaton, 103, 105, 106, 116
immanence, 2
immortality, 55f., 107, 111f.; social, 57
immutable, 15, 18, 128
impassible, 44, 75, 135
indeterminism, 25

individual, God as, 34-43, 64, 65, 78, 136; inexhaustible by a
    definition, 130; integrity of, 6, 46; ordinary, 43f.
individuality, 25; and universality, 34-39; cosmic, 102
individuation, principle of, 68, 77
infinite, God as, 21, 36, 74, 128; possibility as, 24
influence, God as immune to, 44; as open to, 39, 41, 44
integrity, 6, 45f.
interaction, 38ff., 67, 69, 98, 116, 133f.
interactionism, 98
intuition, 24
Islam, 7

James, W., 47
Jesus, 107
Job, 103, 116ff.
Judaism, 7

Kafka, F., 121f.
Kant, E., xi, 25, 26, 27, 28, 32, 33, 48f., 50, 52,
    54, 76, 85
Kepler, J., 91
Kierkegaard, S., 62, 131

language and God, 79
laws of nature, 53, 89
Leibniz, G. W., 115f.
Lequier, J., 113, 115, 127
Longfellow, S., 114
love, 12ff., 17; divine, 45, 56, 75, 104, 107, 110f., 132, 137;
    for God, 8, 108

materialism, 57, 98
Mavrodes, G., 30
Maya, 23
metaphysical, 32
metaphysics, 24, 136
modal coincidence, 20, 21, 72
most real, 71
mystery of God, 77
mystics, 104

natural theology, x, 124, 135; collapse of, 66

necessity of God's existence, 20, 59, 67, 85f., 102
need, absolute, 48; relative, 48
negation, parasitic, 69
negative theology, 70
neoclassical, metaphysics, 81, 134f.; theism, 27, 70, 75, 116
Niebuhr, R., 34
nonfragmentary being, 7, 28, 38
nothing, 83, 89, 106

object, God as, 130
Ogden, S., 126n., 135
omnipotence, 119, 122
omniscience, 12, 83, 85f.
ontological argument, 17, 39, 50, 124
order of world, 53, 59
orderer of nature, 57, 60
organism, 98ff.

panentheism, 135
pantheism, 8, 9
Paul, St., 9, 109
Peirce, C. S., 73, 115
perfection, 18f., 72
Pfleiderer, O., 127, 135
Philo, 17, 28
philosophy, God of, 132
Plato, x, 14, 15, 21, 28, 97, 99, 107, 113, 114f., 125
Plotinus, 24, 28, 106
polytheism, 61
Popper, K., 67
positivist, 40, 51
possible world, 73, 88
potentiality, God's, 20, 71f., 74, 79
power of God, 118ff.
proof, moral, 48f.; nature of, 74, 79; theistic, 45ff.
proofs, classical, 29
purpose, multiple, 59

quantum mechanics, 92

Ramanuja, 97
rational living, requirements of, 49

real, most, 32
reality as ordered, 53
reason, natural, xi; and belief, 31, 32
relations, external, 26f.; internal, 26
relativity, God's, 70; in physics, 93ff.
religion, 2, 102ff.; God of, 132; high, 1, 102
responsiveness, divine, 134
revelation, 77, 103
reward, of virtue, 108; for serving God, 117
ruler, God as, 64, 98
rules applicable to God, 34, 51, 60, 63f., 76
Ryle, G., 63

salvation, 22
Sankara, 23
Sartre, J.-P., 10
satori, 22
Schweitzer, A., 48
self-surpassing, 18ff., 72, 129
service of God, 55
Socinians, 113
soul as self-moved, 115
Sozzini, F., 127
Spinoza, B., 2, 3, 17, 26, 73
substance, 22
suffering in God, 105
summum bonum, 54
supreme being, 34
surpassable, 42
Suzuki, D. T., 22

Tennant, F. R., 67
theism, classical, 41; empirical, 87; neoclassical, **27**
theology, natural, x
Tillich, P., 17, 34f., 62, 85
timeless being, 104, 128
tragedy even for God, 123
transcendent, 114
Trinity, the, 105
truth and value, 47

ubiquitous, 45, 67, 131
unbelievers, 91

unconditioned, 27
uniqueness, conceptual, 69
universal individual, 34ff.
unsurpassability, 17, 39ff., 55, 58, 64, 95, 127, 134

Varisco, B., 113, 115

Weiss, P., 132
Whitehead, A. N., 23, 26, 74, 115
whole, God as, 8, 21
wholeness, 6-17
wishful thinking, 46f.
worship, 3ff., 15, 28, 39, 65, 74, 78, 102, 119, 128